**W9-AQO-231**

# TOWARD
# A SOCIOLOGY
# OF DEATH
# AND DYING

Edited by

## Lyn H. Lofland

**SAGE** PUBLICATIONS    *Beverly Hills / London*    1976

The material in this publication originally appeared as a special issue of URBAN LIFE (Volume 4, Number 3, October 1975). The Publisher would like to acknowledge the assistance of the special issue editor, Lyn H. Lofland, in making this edition possible.

*For information address:*

**SAGE** Publications, Inc.
275 South Beverly Drive
Beverly Hills, California 90212

**SAGE** Publications Ltd
28 Banner Street
London EC1Y 8QE

Printed in the United States of America

International Standard Book Number 0-8039-0586-6

Library of Congress Catalog Card Number 75-32378

THIRD PRINTING

# CONTENTS

# TOWARD A SOCIOLOGY
# OF DEATH AND DYING

*LYN H. LOFLAND* is an assistant professor of sociology at the University of California, Davis. She is a former vice editor of *Urban Life* and the author of *A World of Strangers: Order and Action in Urban Public Space*. She is currently involved in a study of human loss and connection and in analyzing the emergent "death movement."

# TOWARD A SOCIOLOGY OF
# DEATH AND DYING:

*Editor's Introduction*

To ANYONE PAYING ANY ATTENTION at all, it must be obvious that in the past few years, death and dying have become very "in" topics. They are celebrated in college classrooms, in a torrential outpouring of books, in newspapers, magazine and journal articles, in seminars and conferences, in television documentaries and talk shows, and in newly organized or rejuvenated research clearing houses and foundations. Much of the current attention to these topics is, as past attention has been, of an exhortive or ameliorative or speculative character. The more scholarly work has tended to emerge primarily from psychologists and psychiatrists, especially those concerned with suicide or grief. And while sociologists have certainly had a part in this tide of attention, a large, comprehensive, and solid body of materials clearly labeled "sociology of death and dying" has yet to be amassed. There is, for example, to my knowledge, no published, or at least nationally distributed, book of readings devoted exclusively to sociological writings or taking exclusively a sociological perspective. There is only a single recently published text (Vernon, 1970) and the first (apparently) session on "death and dying" ever scheduled at the ASA national meetings took place this year.

I certainly do not mean to suggest that sociological or sociologically relevant studies and analyses do not exist. There is an enormous anthropological literature, of course, and much of the theorizing about such matters as the origin and functions of religion and about the functions of funeral and mourning rituals has had its source in this anthropological data base. Nor have individual sociologists (and anthropologists working in complex societies) been mute. From Durkheim on, social science scholars have, intermittently at least, turned their attention to the fact of death, sometimes for major portions of their professional careers, sometimes only for the duration of a single study or essay.[1] What I am suggesting, rather, is simply that as a well-defined sub-area within the discipline, comparable to stratification or deviance, say, the sociology of death and dying is only now being created.[2]

It is my hope and, I think, that of the authors whose invited work is represented here, that this special issue of *Urban Life* will make some contribution to that creation. Toward the furtherance of that goal, I should like briefly, in the few pages of this introduction, to offer some rather informal and perhaps slightly querulous musings about the current and future "state of the art," and in so doing, provide at least a partial context for interpreting the individual research and analyses reported herein.

\*　　\*　　\*

The seven articles contained in this volume share, it seems to me, three interrelated qualities which allow them, collectively, to counter, or at least qualify, much of the extant conventional wisdom—scholarly and popular—regarding dying and death in contemporary America—qualities in which the best work in the sociology of death (and perhaps in sociology more generally) also partakes and to which the emergent sub-area might well seriously attend. These qualities are a tolerance for complexity, conceptual irreverence, and empirical grounding. Let me consider each in turn.

## A Tolerance for Complexity

Much of what has been and is being written and said relative to death and dying, for scholarly but particularly for lay consumption, has a sweepingly simple character. For example: "Americans fear death and therefore deny it." Or, conversely, "Americans fear death but quite straightforwardly accept it." (See Dumont and Foss, 1972, for a thorough review of this relatively long-standing controversy.) There is something marvelously attractive about such assertions. One does not have to bother to ask what Americans, in what social group, of what age, under what conditions, with what degree of salience, and covering what time period. Just "Americans." One does not have to ask what exactly it means to deny or accept, what actions or opinions or practices indicate one or the other.

One does not have even to consider possibly complex, possibly simultaneously held but contradictory, possibly varying orientations. Just "deny or accept." As another example: it is often asserted that American physicians are emotionally and interactionally inept at handling dying and death because they fear death even more than the average person—which is why they become physicians in the first place. One does not have to ask what physicians, working in what kinds of organizational settings, socialized in what manner, confronting what sorts of situations, and holding what sorts of professional ideologies. Just "physicians." Just "fear and ineptness."

Despite their seductive character, the problem with such sweepingly simple generalizations, as the seven reports contained herein suggest, is that they are likely to be untrue *as stated*. Armed with a tolerance for complexity, researchers who go out to look come back with reports of phenomena far too intricate and varied to be captured adequately by the unqualified simple sentence. Consider, as you read this issue, all the variations in thinking and feeling about and acting toward various sorts of death and dying at various sorts of levels described in the articles by Marshall, Gubrium, Lofland, Charmaz, Matthews, and Wood. Consider the intricacy, explicated by Coombs and Powers, of understanding even that small portion of the physician's experience with death contained within the period of formal training, much less within the years of practice.

Relative only (for brevity's sake) to the acceptance/denial controversy, then, these reports suggest that—rather than asking simply, "Do Americans accept or deny death?" or "Why do Americans accept or deny death?"—it is more fruitful to ask such questions as: What are the various orientations that Americans in varying social locations—class, ethnic, occupational, age, and so forth—hold relative to varying aspects of death and dying under varying conditions? How is the handling of various aspects of dying and death variously organized in various settings? In what way, if at all, do organizational arrangements reflect actors' orientations? Under what conditions do varying patterns of death organization and orientation emerge? What might be the consequences of these? And so on. A tolerance for complexity may make life more complicated for the researcher/analyst, but the reward is surely enriched understanding.

## Conceptual Irreverence

One of the more deadly diseases of the intellectual mind is the tendency to beatify extant concepts. Rather than treating them as tools to be discarded or modified according to their usefulness in interpreting the complexities of the empirical world, they are clung to tenaciously, and the empirical world is discarded or modified to fit them. The papers in this volume are not so inflicted. Instead, they evidence a certain irreverence toward, a freedom with, the tools of the trade. Marshall, for example, borrows Glaser and Strauss' "status passage" whole cloth, because it seems "useful" in explicating his materials; but he freely modifies the sacrosanct "acceptance or denial" in favor of acceptance, resignation, and legitimation. Wood develops her own concept, "scheduled concern," to try to organize and illuminate her materials and takes the Kübler-Ross (1969) formulation of dying "stages" simply as "a belief." And so on from article to article.

Perhaps I can make clearer what I mean by the advantages of conceptual irreverence and the disadvantages of beatification by noting a single disadvantage—that beatification tends to close off rather than open up inquiry—and by illustrating this with the curious case of the concept, taboo. Beginning, perhaps, with Herman Feifel's (1963) article on "Death" in Norman Farberow's edited book, *Taboo Topics,* the assertion that death is a taboo topic in America has been repeated so often, by so many people, in so many contexts, that one begins to believe it must surely, somewhere, be engraved on stone—the revealed words of the gods.[3] The problem with this assertion and with the concept, taboo, is that once stated, once utilized, there is very little else left to do. One can ask why death is taboo, of course, but that is about the limit of possible inquiry. If death is a taboo topic, people simply don't talk about it, and there is really nothing more to say about the matter. But if one takes a certain irreverent attitude toward this concept, if one is unconvinced that conversational realities are fully contained by it, one can begin "doing" a great deal. One can begin asking such questions as these: Under what conditions and with whom do varying persons discuss varying aspects of death? What historic changes have there been, if any, in the zones of appropriateness for death talk? Under what conditions will death talk of what sort reach the public discourse, and under what conditions will it be confined to private discussion? Do varying cultures and subcultures or specific social locations provide more or less support for death talk of various sorts? And so forth and so on.

While none of the articles contained herein directly confronts or challenges the taboo concept (and several assume its applicability), it is nonetheless clear from *what the authors are doing* that none of them is taking it too seriously. Because what they are doing, in large measure, is listening (directly or through the historic record) and recording what people in varying social locations under varying organizational conditions are *saying* or *not saying* about death: other people's, their own, in general. And in this irreverence, they have begun to supply materials which can begin to answer some of the questions suggested above.

## Empirical Grounding

This third quality is intimately related to those already discussed, as those have been to one another. By empirical grounding I refer not only to the careful empirical work which made possible the analyses contained in this volume, but also to the way in which the authors have *grounded* their empirical assertions in time, place, organizational arrangements, groups, and so forth. The reader will discover here few of those unqualified sweeping generalizations found so disconcertingly often in writings about death, which imply (as much by what they don't say as by what they do) that a human universal has been unearthed (for example, people fear death, funerals function to discharge grief, unexpressed grief emerges in pathological symptoms, dying persons move through [five] or [six] or [nine] or [whatever] stages). This grounding may be in broad historical terms, as with Lofland's analysis of state executions, or it may be locationally and temporally specific, as with Gubrium's delineation of the three worlds of death coexisting within a single nursing home. The tie-in may be to organizational or occupational settings (as in the pieces by Wood, Coombs and Powers, Charmaz, and Marshall) or it may be to aggregate persons who share little more than certain common traits (as in Matthews' discussion of old women facing death). But whatever its precise character, the empirical grounding of these studies repeatedly emphasizes the complex interrelations between actors, orientations, actions, time, setting, and structure. And in so doing, it lays bare the simplistic overstatement and the beatified concept for the distortions they truly are.

\* \* \*

These seven papers do not, of course, cover the full range of *concrete* (much less, analytic) topics which might be of interest to a sociology of death and dying.[4] In none of the articles is the major concern with such matters as mourning, death rituals, body disposal, conceptions of after-life, mass death, reform movements relative to death and dying, grief, the mortuary industry, the experience of widows and widowers, death humor, consequences of changing death rates, or cemeteries, to mention just a few. But as I noted at the outset, the qualities which these reports share in their consideration of the topics which *are* covered may well suggest a fruitful approach for future research on those topics which are not.

—*Lyn H. Lofland*
University of California, Davis

## NOTES

1. See, for example, Blauner, 1966; Dumont and Foss, 1972; Eliot, 1930 and 1932-1933; Fulton, 1961 and 1964; Glaser and Strauss, 1965 and 1968; Glick, Weiss, and Parkes, 1974; Habenstein and Lamers, 1955 and 1960; Lopata, 1973; Parsons, 1963; Parsons and Lidz, 1967; Pine and Phillips, 1970; Sudnow, 1967; Vernon, 1970; Wallace, 1973; and Warner, 1959, for a small sampling of this material.

2. One might argue that, as a substantive rather than analytic topic, the sociology of death and dying ought not be created at all—that its unique materials ought, as they have largely in the past, simply be grist for the mill of analysts of micro-interaction or organizational processes or stratification, or whatever. While I am attracted by the tidy logic of such an arrangement, I am also cognizant of the fact that the emergence of sociological sub-specialties has not heretofore been guided to any noticeable degree by logic. The field is a hodgepodge of specialties at varying and overlapping and confusing levels of abstraction. The principle that sociology *is* what sociologists *do* seems sufficient justification for adding to the confusion. I should note also that while there is considerable overlap in personnel and interests between "death and dying" and medical sociology, the latter by no means can be said to contain the former.

3. The constant and unequivocal reiteration of this assertion appears, recently, to be abating—perhaps because it has come to be seen as somewhat incongruous for large numbers of people to be talking and writing to large numbers of people about a topic which nobody talks about.

4. Several of the pieces do, however, touch tangentially on areas which are not their primary focus—Charmaz's materials, for example, might be useful in thinking about grief and mourning; Wood's, in thinking about the dying role or identity.

## REFERENCES

BLAUNER, R. (1966) "Death and social structure." Psychiatry 29: 378-394.
DUMONT, R. G. and D. C. FOSS (1972) The American View of Death: Acceptance or Denial? Cambridge, Mass.: Shenkman.
ELIOT, T. (1932-1933) "A step toward the social psychology of bereavement." J. of Abnormal & Social Psychology 27: 380-390.

——— (1930) "The adjustive behavior of bereaved families; a new field for research." Social Forces 8 (June): 543-549.

FEIFEL, H. (1963) "Death," pp. 8-21 in N. Farberow (ed.) Taboo Topics. New York: Atherton.

FULTON, R. L. (1964) "Death and the self." J. of Religion & Health 3: 359-368.

——— (1961) "The clergyman and the funeral director: a study in role conflict." Social Forces 39 (May): 317-323.

GLASER, B. and A. STRAUSS (1968) Time for Dying. Chicago: Aldine.

——— (1965) Awareness of Dying. Chicago: Aldine.

GLICK, I. O., R. S. WEISS, and C. M. PARKES (1974) The First Year of Bereavement. New York: John Wiley.

HABENSTEIN, R. and W. M. LAMERS (1960) Funeral Customs the World Over. Milwaukee: Bulfin Printers.

——— (1955) The History of American Funeral Directing. Milwaukee: Bulfin Printers.

KUBLER-ROSS, E. (1969) On Death and Dying. New York: Macmillan.

LOPATA, H. Z. (1973) Widowhood in an American City. Cambridge, Mass.: Schenkman.

PARSONS, T. (1963) "Death in American society—a brief working paper." Amer. Behavioral Scientist 6 (May): 61-65.

——— and V. LIDZ (1967) "Death in American society," pp. 133-170 in E. Shneidman (ed.) Essays in Self-Destruction. New York: Science House.

PINE, V. R. and D. PHILLIPS (1970) "The cost of dying: a sociological analysis of funeral expenditure." Social Problems (Winter): 405-417.

SUDNOW, D. (1967) Passing On: The Social Organization of Dying. Englewood Cliffs, N.J.: Prentice-Hall.

VERNON, G. (1970) Sociology of Death: An Analysis of Death-Related Behavior. New York: Ronald Press.

WALLACE, S. (1973) After Suicide. New York: John Wiley.

WARNER, W. L. (1959) The Living and the Dead. New Haven: Yale Univ. Press.

*ROBERT H. COOMBS* is Associate Research Sociologist and Chief of the Camarillo-Neuropsychiatric Institute Research Program in the Department of Psychiatry, University of California, Los Angeles. His book-length works include *Psychosocial Aspects of Medical Training, Socialization in Drug Abuse,* and *Junkies and Straights: The Camarillo Experience.* Soon to be published is *Students into Doctors: Professional Socialization in Medical School.*

*PAULINE S. POWERS* is Assistant Professor of Psychiatry at the University of South Florida in Tampa. She received her M.D. degree from the University of Iowa. Her research interests include social psychiatry and the study of thought disorder in psychotic patients.

## SOCIALIZATION FOR DEATH:

### The Physician's Role

### ROBERT H. COOMBS
### PAULINE S. POWERS

IN DAYS GONE BY, death was a family experience. In the hamlets and villages of rural America, people usually died at home attended by family members and friends of long acquaintance. At the moment of death, these intimate associates were often present, providing comforting care, exchanging meaningful words, and then observing the termination of breathing and the total relaxation of the body.[1]

In striking contrast, death in the contemporary urban setting now occurs primarily in hospitals and other medical facilities. Only rarely are family members or friends present during the final moments of life. Instead, the dying are attended by medical and paramedical specialists, each highly trained to perform technical services in combating disease and death. Presiding over this staff of technical experts is the attending physician. He is the commander-in-chief, the one authoritative

*AUTHORS' NOTE:* This research was supported by grants from the National Institute on Mental Health (MH 15454 and MH 19292) and from the National Fund for Medical Education (884-348).

figure recognized by others as inevitably concerned with dying and death. Not only does he orchestrate the clinical efforts of staff, but he is also required by his presiding role to decide when the patient is dead (an increasingly complex decision), to sign the death certificate, and then to confront the family with the news.

It is no easy matter to learn this difficult role successfully, for potentially conflicting demands are often placed upon the physician.[2] He is not only expected to be expert in applying highly specialized technical skills, but he also must treat the patient—and his family—with gentleness and sympathy. His main job is to cure if possible, but he must also relieve and comfort. All of medicine's scientific advances have not eliminated the patient's need for warm sensitivity and understanding concern.

But the doctor cannot take death and dying too personally: he is expected to retain composure, no matter how dramatic or tragic the death scene might be. Rationality and clearness of judgment in moments of grave peril must characterize his every action. The physician who loses coolness and presence of mind also loses the confidence of patients and staff. Clearly, a doctor sobbing over a favorite patient is no doctor at all.

## STUDYING THE SOCIALIZATION OF PHYSICIANS

To understand how physicians-in-training master the complexities of the clinical role pertaining to death and dying, we have utilized extensive data derived from longitudinal interviews and participant observation. The primary source of information comes from a panel analysis of an entire class of medical students who entered medical school in the fall of 1967 and exited in June 1971 with the M.D. degree. During each year of training, members of the class were interviewed about their changing attitudes toward death and dying.[3] Two hundred and twenty-nine tape-recorded interviews, of a possible 239, were obtained, all but two of which were personally conducted by the senior author. These interviews were transcribed, coded, and tabulated.

Enriching these longitudinal data are field notes derived from participant observation at the medical school and teaching hospital. By accompanying students as they went about their activities, additional insights were generated to supplement the interview information. These observations were in turn checked against the observations of the second author, who only recently had personally experienced the status passage through successive stages of medical training—medical school, internship, and residency. The second author also conducted tape-recorded interviews with 13 of her medical colleagues.[4] These intensive interviews not only provided insights concerning socialization experiences during the latter stages of training (that is, internship and residency), but also gave retrospective views of how medical training affects later clinical practice.

## DEVELOPMENTAL STAGES IN DEALING WITH DEATH

In the medical school and teaching hospital, medical aspirants learn the physician's role. Here recruits are processed through a series of challenging experiences which, if encountered successfully, transform them from laymen into effective physicians. Described in sociological terms, the medical center is a formal socializing system whose function it is to prepare participants for the physician's role—a role which requires considerable expertise in dealing with death and dying.[5]

Our thesis is that, in learning to deal with this sensitive subject, medical practitioners evolve through fairly predictable developmental stages. While these stages are not inevitable, we suggest that they are representative of the developmental changes which typically occur as laymen change into seasoned clinical practitioners.

## Stage I: Idealizing the Doctor's Role

Upon beginning medical training, students have essentially the same attitudes and feelings about death as the general public. Having had little personal experience with death and dying, students are no more enlightened than others. Like laymen, they regard the doctor as a bulwark against death and suffering. In their minds, death is the antithesis of good medical practice. "That's my business," a freshman said, "to make sure death doesn't occur."

Emotionally, too, beginning students differ little from laymen in the way they respond to death. They have not escaped the fears and phobias which beset others. Obviously, death can be a shocking experience, and students are not immune to the normal emotional reactions which occur on such occasions. To deal routinely with dying people, as they must learn to do, requires coping skills which they have not yet developed.[6]

At this pre-professional stage, personal identification with dying patients is strong, especially if the latter are young and likable, and students are apt to find themselves participating imaginatively in the suffering involved. They have not yet evolved from the layman's attitude toward suffering and death. In time, however, they will begin to acquire the detachment and equanimity of the veteran doctor, which many of them realize. Nonetheless, this transition can be quite painful. Intellectual understanding is one thing, but managing feelings is quite another.

Initially, students find the coolness of the case-hardened clinician offensive. In their idealistic view, the physician, like the proverbial country doctor, should be warm and compassionate. So it is disillusioning to witness the detachment which is typically exhibited in the hospital setting. For example, when one freshman was given an opportunity to accompany upperclassmen on ward rounds, he was appalled by the "unfeeling way" the attending physician talked to the group about a terminally ill patient. "I'd sure hate to have the family hear him talk like that," he said. "I suppose the doctor has to be uncompassionate at times, but I wasn't ready for it. He wasn't disrespectful, but he just didn't show any emotion."

Similarly, a sophomore was shocked at the detached attitude of the staff about the death of his first patient. Unaware of her death, he had tried to locate her in the hospital room and was told matter of factly, "She's in the morgue." "This really bothered me," he confessed. "I went to her autopsy and it made me think pretty deeply for awhile."

Another student was appalled by the scientific interest displayed by the clinical staff who attended his first patient, a baby who was unsuccessfully operated on for a congenital cardiac anomaly: "The surgeon was sorry, I guess, but it was kind of a scientific study to him; things like this evidently happen every week or two." Later, during the autopsy, this student was stunned when the pediatric cardiologist was "real excited when the autopsy findings compared well with his own diagnosis."

Upsetting as these experiences are, most students realize, at least on an intellectual level, that such detachment does not necessarily indicate a lack of concern, and that, in fact, a doctor's failure to become emotionally involved may be in the best interests of the patient. Later on, in fact, these same students may find themselves reacting to death much like their mentors, but at this initial stage they typically respond as do laymen.

## Stage II: Desensitizing Death Symbols

From the beginning of medical training, students are conditioned in the art of remaining emotionally aloof in the face of human tragedy. In medical practice, death is omnipresent, and the prospective doctor must be desensitized to its symbols— blood, bones, corpses, and stench—symbols which are disturbing to most people.[7] Although many students have had some desensitizing experiences in their pre-med courses which require them to dissect and sometimes even kill living things, medical school experiences can be shocking.

Almost the moment students arrive in medical school, they are escorted into the anatomy laboratory and introduced to a cadaver, a dead body which they are expected to cut into and dissect in careful detail. Not surprisingly, most students initially feel shock and revulsion upon seeing a room full of dead bodies lying lifeless and gray on steel tables. Few, if any, can carry off such a confrontation with complete sang-froid. Rather, the initial reaction is typically marked by a sense of nausea triggered by the heavy smell of formaldehyde, a sense of recoil upon finding the corpse so cold and rigid to first touch, and a feeling of depression, a loss of appetite, and an inability to concentrate after the first encounter.

But no matter how great the initial shock, it apparently wears off rapidly since most students claim to adjust quickly. Only three of our cohort indicated that more than a week was required to reestablish their emotional equilibrium. Of the latter, one experienced severe anxiety, another was not able to touch the cadaver until he had put on rubber gloves, and the third sought medical treatment for an allergic reaction.

It is not long, however, until students become so desensitized that they can eat their lunches around the corpse. It is important to realize, though, that the ability to undergo such experiences without betraying disgust or squeamishness is a valued characteristic among prospective doctors. This desire to portray nonchalance, to remain "cool," no doubt causes students to exaggerate the ease with which discomforting experiences are met and, in turn, to suppress openness about personal anxieties. The fact that students frequently have bad dreams about the cadaver experience suggests that they do have repressed anxieties.[8]

To manage these anxieties and thereby make the experience more tolerable, students utilize a number of coping mechanisms. One is humor, a ready tension release.[9] Despite faculty efforts to discourage pranks and horseplay, amusing stories about the cadaver circulate among students. They jokingly give amusing names to the lifeless forms, or contrive the body in such a way as to get a laugh—for example, arranging an erect penis on a female student's cadaver. Such antics function as a tension release and also help students forget the morose aspects of the experience.

The challenge to the neophyte doctor is, of course, to keep his personal sensitivities intact while dissecting a human body. Humanistically inclined students, those most prone to worrying about the moral justifications of carving into a cadaver, find relief in the knowledge that patients have willingly donated their own bodies to be used in training medical students.

Inner relief is most typically derived, though, by losing oneself in the details of the work. The pressure to learn myriad body parts in a limited time reinforces the tendency among students to occupy themselves with the finite details of the dissection process and in memorizing the scientific names of bones, muscles, nerves, and other body parts. In so doing, dissection becomes a mechanistic exercise rather than a humanistic experience. This absorption in work clearly acts, to use Lief and Fox's term (1963), as a "psychic non-irritant."

Further desensitization occurs in the second year when students are introduced to pathology and experience their first autopsy. One might suppose this experience to be little different from the cadaver experience. But an autopsy brings students much closer to the subjective or personal aspects of death because the body, only a few hours earlier, was living![10] So it is much easier to identify with the deceased. This personal involvement is enhanced by the fact that, as compared with a cadaver, the body is left heavily draped and appears much more lifelike. Moreover, unlike the cadaver experience, students have knowledge of the patient's identity and medical history through reading the patient's chart and listening to the doctor's report about the fatal illness.

In order to maintain equanimity and protect themselves from the discomfort of such a stressful experience, students, like their mentors, adopt a detached scientific attitude. That is, emotionality is avoided or suppressed by focusing on the

technical aspects of their work. Losing oneself in the pathological details of an autopsy helps prospective doctors maintain
an "objective professional response." Clearly, thinking about
diseased tissue is less emotionally involving than pondering
about the patient as a person.

Required basic-science courses in the freshman and sophomore years provide the scientific terminology and knowledge
necessary for dealing with illness on an intellectual rather than
an emotional basis. Through constant exposure to scientific
aspects of disease, these courses desensitize students to disease
processes, the precursors of death. Reflecting on such a course,
a physician said, "It's just hours and hours of looking at slides
of people who have various illnesses at progressive stages. It's
like looking at war scenes again and again until after a while it
doesn't have the same emotional content."

At this stage, then, the prospective doctor is prepared,
psychologically, to deal with the aversive symbols of death
without displaying emotionality (fear, revulsion, and so forth).
By becoming desensitized to blood, bones, and other symbols
of death which normally elicit uncomfortable feelings, he comes
closer to the expected professional response—a calm, objective
rationality and a full control of emotion. This conditioning
prepares him for the face-to-face encounters he will have with
living patients.

### Stage III: Objectifying and Combating Death

When the training scene shifts from the lecture room and
laboratory to the hospital, students are exposed to some of
life's most poignant dramas. Everywhere present are the
companions of death—pain, suffering, fear, and despair. Here
students learn to distance themselves emotionally from the
living as well as the dead.

Early experiences with dying patients make clear the necessity of detaching oneself from the emotional trauma of death.
"It's really hard the first two or three times a patient dies," a
senior student explained; "so you learn to develop a protective

shield to reduce the emotional impact." Consider, for example, the strain that this stressful experience might have on a fledgling doctor:

> My first patient was a little boy suffering from incurable leukemia. He was all right when he left the hospital, but in about two weeks he came into the emergency room in shock and died three hours later. When I was in the room with him, the attending physician asked, "Who had this patient before?" When I told him I had, he sent me to look after the mother who was crying in the next room. While the doctor worked on the little 5-year-old, I tried to talk to the mother. I really felt terribly inadequate; there wasn't a whole lot I could say to make her feel better. Then we went into the room where they were treating the boy. He was screaming and crying and then stopped breathing. The mother collapsed and somebody caught her. That experience really got to me!

Such happenings make clear to students the necessity of developing coping mechanisms which will allow them to do their work without getting "all wrapped up" in the patients' lives. The main depersonalizing technique, modeled effectively by the clinical faculty, is to objectify death, or, conversely, deny the subjective features. In other words, the clinician learns to view dying patients not as people with feelings, but as medical entities, specimens, or objects of scientific interest. By adopting a scientific frame of mind, utilized so effectively in their previous work with dead bodies, clinicians can effectively avoid the uncomfortable inner feelings which occur when they are exposed to dying patients. In this way, as a fourth-year student points out, "Death can be as neutral as reading the obituary section of the newspaper."[11]

The dynamics by which clinicians dissociate themselves involve an intellectual dissection of the patient into parts and then concentrating on and treating only the pathological part rather than the "whole person." "This is the old scientific fragmentalization method," an experienced physician explained. "You just bust up the human organism into pieces and deal only with the pieces. Then you don't have to see the whole picture." It is this orientation which expresses itself in such comments as "the liver in room 724" or "an interesting case of leukemia."

Obviously there is much less discomfort for a physician in the "expiration" of a "case" than in the death of a patient. Similarly, the "emotional horror" of dealing with a 9-year-old boy dying from a head injury is less stressful, as one physician acknowledged, when concentrating on the anatomy and physiological processes. "That's the model that was driven into me," he recalled.

This is not to say, however, that doctors take lightly their clinical responsibilities. On the contrary, heavy demands are routinely made upon medical trainees to be exhaustively thorough in trying to keep people alive and well. Before a person dies there is usually a "mad scramble," as one put it, to get everything possible done to save him. When a patient stops breathing or his heart stops beating, an emergency announcement is made in code language over the hospital P.A. system ("Code Red, Room 227," for example); this alarm alerts physicians and other specialists of an imminent death. Every available physician is then expected to rush to the bedside of the dying patient. Special emergency squads race through the halls, and the patient is hooked up to monitors and life-saving machinery which elicit a variety of visual and auditory signals. "It's a frantic, noisy, confused state," said one physician; "people in white clothing hurry about knocking themselves out to keep the patient alive." Not until every life-saving attempt has been exhausted do they let up. In the hospital setting, such extraordinary efforts to revive the patient and prolong life are routine.[1][2]

Although members of the medical staff rarely give verbal praise for a job well done, they are fiercely critical of haphazard clinical performance. Clinical pathology conferences, called CPCs or "death rounds," provide a forum for this expression. Whenever a patient dies, the residents, interns, attending staff, and others gather in an auditorium to discuss the "case." Whoever was responsible for the patient presents the clinical history and then the pathology report is given. Everyone then discusses what should have been done differently to avoid the death. "This gave me the idea," one physician said, "that if we were just smarter and had not made this or that mistake the patient would still be alive." Clearly, the assumption is that death is preventable and is not supposed to happen to good physicians. At least, this is the idea that is "handed down" to medical trainees. No wonder a sense of personal defeat is felt when patients die.

At this stage of training, then, death is viewed as the enemy, the opponent, something waiting to snatch away the patient. "The whole idea of medical training," said one physician, "is to teach doctors how to avoid death at almost any cost." So the battle lines are drawn, with death lurking in the shadows in mortal conflict with the physician, attired appropriately in white. At stake is not only the patient's life, but also the clinician's reputation and self-esteem.

### Stage IV: Questioning the Medical Model[13]

With increasing experience, some clinicians begin to question and then to reject the prominent values espoused in medical training about death and dying.[14] The medical teaching model, as these physicians come to perceive it, tends to dehumanize the patient and to make a mere technician out of the doctor. That is, it glorifies the science of medicine (a thorough knowledge of disease processes and a ready command of clinical technique) at the expense of the art of medicine (an interpersonal ability to meet the patient's needs by relating warmly and meaningfully to him and his family). In the physician's quest to master the science of medicine, he comes to regard the patient as an object or thing rather than as a fellow human being. "I hate to admit it," one physician reflected, "but I had come to view the patient almost as an extension of the apparatus in the room."

When death is viewed as the enemy, it is easy to overdo things, to go to extremes in prolonging life. "We would just go on forever," one confessed, "unless someone stopped us." Reflecting back, another physician came to the conclusion that he had become so imbued with the idea of combating death that medical practice had become "a contest between me and the disease; the patient was merely an object over which we were fighting."

The turning point comes when those who reach this questioning stage can no longer escape the absurd extremes to which efforts are sometimes taken to keep patients alive. An intern, for example, was appalled by the efforts of his associates to prolong the life of a 17-year-old boy who had accidentally had part of his head shot off. Despite the fact that the boy had no cerebrum and was doomed to a vegetable-like existence, they wouldn't let him die. Instead, they kept him alive for several years, running up an enormous hospital and medical bill. Throughout all of this, his distraught mother daily put cream on his bedsores at a cost of $80 a bottle. "They were just prolonging a horrible state of affairs," he realized, "because nobody would accept the finality of it. It was kind of a personal failure to let him die."

One physician, who was an exemplary model of his former indoctrination, always worked fiercely to do his duty in combating death. On one occasion, for example, after an unsuccessful effort to resuscitate an elderly man, he became angry when the deceased patient's priest, who was waiting with the family in the adjoining room, acted as though death was a welcome blessing. Although the doctor said nothing at the time, he confessed, "I got angry as hell at him."

One day, though, a particularly harrowing experience "got to" him, and, in those brief hours, he came to question the values implicit in the medical model. For example, after 19 years of general practice, he admitted to the hospital an aging lady of about 75 with her fourth myocardial infarction. During the night she "died" five times and was resuscitated four. During the fourth resuscitation, the weary physician reflected on the "scene of wild chaos" and wondered, "What the hell are we doing to this poor lady? This is no way to die." He recalled, "Here was this little old lady lying spread-eagled across the bed with her tongue hanging out of one side of her mouth and a tube in the other and I thought to myself, 'Why?' " Then, answering his own question, he thought, "Because we haven't guts enough to stop, that's why." This conclusion was reinforced when for the fourth time he bore the news of resuscitation to the daughter who was waiting outside. Rather than thanking him for his heroic effort, the heartsick woman simply looked at him and, in a pleading voice, said "Please. . . ."

Such experiences stimulate some physicians to question whether their efforts to avoid death at any cost are really appropriate; and some eventually come to believe, as one said, that, in certain instances, people have "a right to die." "I have gotten beyond the stage concerned about technique and the notion that death implies failure," one practicing doctor said. "I've come to accept the fact that death is not the enemy, not something that must be conquered by the physician. People have a right to die in peace and dignity."

The extraordinary efforts to keep some patients functioning are seen by such doctors as "just so much medical pyrotechnics," designed to fulfill the physician's own needs rather than those of the patient and his family. One said, "The function of medical heroics is to demonstrate how good we are with our fancy gadgets; a good doctor can win recognition by keeping the poor old body going forever." In other words, professional recognition and self-esteem come to a physician by demonstrating technical ability (for instance, the ability to perform an appendectomy with only a buttonhole scar). But not much recognition comes from one's colleagues by being known as a warm and kind clinician who is compassionate and sympathetic.

A doctor's ego is easily inflated when he is cast in the role of the healer with power over death. When patients must entrust their lives to the physician, they naturally want to believe in his healing powers. Placed on a pedestal, he can easily feel omnipotent and become intoxicated with a sense of his own powers.[15] When his self-esteem is involved, it is imperative that he prevent death from occurring, for death makes him feel vulnerable. But if he can keep the "corpse" alive for a few more days or weeks, his mastery over death is demonstrated. "He's not about to let his omnipotence be challenged if he can help it," said one; "but if you talk to the family, you'll find that they are usually sorry that the patient had to suffer those extra days and that the hospital bill ran up so high."

As physicians at this stage view it, "the God complex" is incompatible with good medical practice. In their view it is unrealistic to expect a cure for everybody and inappropriate in many situations to unnecessarily prolong life. After all, death is, sooner or later, inevitable for everyone. In the final analysis, then, one cannot control death but can only temporarily delay it for shorter or longer periods, as the case may be. In this larger view the physician is, in reality, only a humble bystander.

Physicians who have reached this stage perceive a good clinician to be one who has mastered the art as well as the science of medicine, an achievement which was aptly summarized by the physician who said, "In the medical profession there are lots of doctors [i.e., technicians], but only relatively few physicians." It is the latter who, rather than possessing a compulsive concern for demonstrating clinical mastery over death, deem it imperative to consider the feelings of the patient and his family.

## Stage V: Dealing with Personal Feelings

Up to this point their experience has conditioned clinicians to repress or suppress personal anxieties and fears about death. Everyone knows that the good doctor is supposed to be calm, with his own feelings under control—someone on whom the family can rely for steady support, insight, and understanding. The doctor who feels anxiety or fear in the face of death must carefully conceal these emotions. "I've had a lot of training in putting up a good front so that others can't see what I'm feeling inside," one said. "I've learned to keep this cool facade of being in control, but inside I'm feeling a lot of stress."

Our interviews with physicians revealed rather dramatically how much suppressed emotionality exists among medical practitioners. When probed, most of them disclosed unresolved psychic problems, some of which create severe stress. During our interviews, several wept. A research note by the interviewer indicates, "These interviews are getting markedly more difficult. Everybody I've talked to so far is having a horrible time dealing with death and dying; and it isn't just on a professional level, but personally, too." Surprisingly, one physician unmasked a phobia of death. "I'm really horrified by looking at or being near dead bodies," he said. Throughout medical training and practice, this physician had tried to avoid the presence of corpses but, of course, this was not always possible. So he had experienced some extremely stressful times, as one might imagine.

His phobia stemmed from a childhood experience at the funeral of his father, a scene which has lingered with him throughout the years.

> I walked up to the coffin and was startled by this awful, mottled, purple-looking face. They hadn't done a very good job of preserving and embalming him. After all of these years I still wake up at night and am actually scared to open my eyes because I can see my father—the dead figure—standing in a corner. I tell myself, "Hey, you're being silly," but I haven't got rid of it yet.

Tragically, not once during the entire period of this troubled physician's medical training did any mentor provide an opportunity for him to ventilate his fears and anxieties. Although he has developed ample technical skills and is now recognized as an accomplished physician, he is, in part, by his own admission, emotionally crippled.

Other physicians, too, revealed anxieties related to the personal loss of loved ones, the sense of helplessness in dealing with hopeless diseases, and the disquieting experience of inadvertently "killing" a patient through error or bad advice. For instance, one physician, while yet an intern, had this traumatic experience:

> A woman came in with severe ascites and I did a paracentesis on her. As we were getting the fluid she went into shock and died. At the

"post" we found that the trochar had gone through an aberrant major artery in the abdominal wall. This shook me up pretty badly. Although it wasn't done deliberately, I had actually killed somebody. I felt very upset!

Although his technical procedures were critically reviewed in the death conference, no one gave the heartsick doctor any help with regard to his emotions. Instead, like other medical trainees, he was left to work out his feelings on his own.

Until physicians reach this stage of self-examination, they often cope with impending death by utilizing avoidance as a technique. "I try to keep away from patients if I know what's coming up so as to reduce the emotional stress," a medical student confessed. Feelings of helplessness stimulated by hopelessly ill patients can be relieved by passing these patients off to someone else or by being too busy to spend much time with them. When contact must be made by the physician, he can simply check the equipment, write the orders and say, "Hi! How are you feeling?" then bustle off to see someone else.[16] "We ignore the patient because we are so fearful ourselves," one commented.[17]

Typically every effort is made in the hospital setting to shield oneself from mourning relatives. In the emergency room quiet crying is tolerated, but if any kind of emotional outburst occurs, relatives are usually hustled off to the chapel as fast as possible. "We isolate them so that their grief is not so obvious," a physician said. "It isn't done cruelly, but, frankly, it is done more to protect the emergency room staff than to help the family."

The physician transcends this stage of avoidance as he begins to realize that how one feels inside is much more important than what is actually being said and done. Self-examination is stimulated when, in trying to be more than a mere technician, he tries to deal meaningfully with the feelings of patients and their families. If he is truly to assist others in more than a technical sense, a doctor must come to grips with his own feelings. How can he allay others' fears and anxieties if he denies the inevitability of death or fails to acknowledge his own mortality? Is it realistic to expect comforting relief from one who in his own training has had such little supportive help in dealing with his own feelings?

Reflecting back upon their earlier training, physicians at this stage fault their mentors for giving them such little help with the subjective aspects of death. "It's almost as though I've had to deal with this part of medical practice without being prepared for it," one said. "In most every other aspect of my training, I've had a chance to observe my preceptors and then discuss the experience." On the topic of death, however, medical trainees are left to their own common sense assumptions. The few who were fortunate enough to receive some instruction on this topic characterized the pedagogical experience as being intellectualized and abstract. The topic of how to handle a dying patient was dealt with, one said, "in cookbook-like fashion, no different than if we were learning to work up a case of hypertension." Another pointed out, "We were never asked to express our feelings or discuss how we felt about death." Nor could any physician recall a single experience where a clinical mentor openly revealed his own feelings about death—the frustrations, anger, or feelings of hopelessness that occur when a patient dies. So each medical trainee is left to his own resources in resolving inner dilemmas on this sensitive subject.

The result of this unhappy state of affairs is, as has been indicated, that until he does come to grips with his feelings, the doctor tends to depersonalize the patient or, failing that, to avoid him and his family. And, as previously mentioned, the system of recognition and rewards which operates in the medical milieu reinforces the tendency to be analytical and nonemotional. "I can speak for myself and possibly for a lot of other physicians," one practicing doctor said. "In my younger years my professional self-image wouldn't permit me to be slowed down or have my efficiency reduced by my feelings. So I evolved into a condition of what I now call 'disembodied intelligence.' But now I'm trying to get more and more in touch with my own feelings, to recognize and tolerate them, and thereby be in a better position to help others with their feelings."

Once having reached this stage, the introspective physician who has recognized his own feelings and limitations, and has managed to reconcile them as well, is uniquely capable of practicing compleat medicine. He alone has the personal ability and resources to bring technical knowledge and sympathetic care to dying patients and their loved ones.

## CONCLUSION

The career path to physicianhood is a well-marked route. One begins as a freshman medical student and then advances to successive stages of sophomore, junior, and then senior. After medical school graduation, the fledgling doctor becomes an intern, then a resident, and, finally, a private practitioner.[18] During this long journey, medical aspirants undergo a variety of personally challenging experiences, not the least of which is dealing with dying patients and their families. [9]

At the journey's outset medical recruits are no better prepared for dealing with death than their contemporaries, and initially they respond as laymen. Inexperienced and idealistic, many become disillusioned, with 5 to 10% dropping out, many during the first year (Gough and Hall, 1975). Those who press forward must develop emotional calluses; they must become accustomed to dealing with stressful circumstances, such as death, which normally are upsetting. The fact that their patients expect them to be sympathetic and compassionate, as well as technically competent, is no small challenge. Yet the development and maintenance of this delicate balance is the test of true skill in fulfilling the physician's role.

Longitudinal observations make clear the social processes which condition rookie clinicians to handle death and dying with rationality and composure. However, the educational processes which foster empathy and compassion are not clearly visible. Death is a daily occurrence in the teaching hospital, but talk about death as a stressful human vicissitude is almost nonexistent.

Medical educators seem no less inhibited in their ability to verbalize feelings about death than the lay public.[20] As the socializing system now operates, if a medical journeyman is to come to grips with his own feelings so that he can interact comfortably with dying patients in this awesome yet ubiquitous experience, he must do it on his own. Unfortunately this self-analysis does not always happen to those who travel the career pathway.[21]

La Rochefoucauld has said, "One cannot look directly at either the sun or death" (Lifton and Olson, 1974). Due to this human frailty, a wall of silence often surrounds the dying patient at a time when feelings cry for expression. The very facts from which the patient is usually shielded are the same ones that he is forced to live and die with, and quite alone.[22] As commander-in-chief at the death scene, an event which now typically occurs in hospitals and extended care settings rather than in the familiar setting of one's own home, the physician has great potential for rendering healing aid in a spiritual or humanistic as well as a technical sense. The doctor is in a unique position to ease the fear, alienation, and loneliness of the dying patient. But if his mastery of the healing arts includes only an ability to patch up and keep the body functioning, he leaves unfulfilled the yearnings of the human soul at one of life's most dramatic and important moments.[23]

The developmental personality changes which result from medical socialization, as now constituted, are not conducive to preparing the doctor emotionally so that he can meet the needs of dying patients and their families in the depersonalized hospital setting. Little recognition currently exists among medical educators that the doctor's role is more than that of gatekeeper of the nation's health—that, in fact, he also presides over the death scene.[24] If he is to fulfill the role which is increasingly expected of him, he must be better prepared to deal with the subjective features of this poignant experience.

# NOTES

1. For background information concerning the cultural roots of death orientations in American society, see Parsons and Lidz (1967).

2. For a discussion of the competing demands inherent in the doctor's role, see Merton (1957), especially pp. 73-79.

3. The topic of death and dying was but one of many covered during the interviews, which varied in length from 1.5 to 3 hours, depending on student loquatiousness. More than 200 items of information were included in the recorded questions and answers. Results of the larger study will soon be published in a book entitled *Students into Doctors: Professional Socialization in Medical School* (by R. H. Coombs, in preparation).

4. Interviews were conducted on the West Coast before Dr. Powers accepted her present position. The 13 physicians interviewed ranged in age from 30 to 57, with a mean age of 41. Three were women, ten were men, and all but one, an anesthesiologist, were currently in psychiatric training or in the private practice of psychiatry. The physicians interviewed have a wide variety of experience. Eight were in general practice prior to beginning psychiatric training; among these the average length of general practice was 12 years, with a range of from 2 to 25 years. One physician interviewed had been an anesthesiologist for 7 years. Two physicians who took part in the study had been in the service after internship and prior to psychiatric training. The two physicians remaining had gone directly through psychiatric training. One of the physicians was a minister and one was a social worker prior to going to medical school. Ten of the 13 physicians interviewed went to medical school in the United States, and three were trained in foreign countries.

5. A further discussion on the topic of the medical center as a social system is given by Bloom (1971).

6. An earlier report about the coping mechanisms utilized by seasoned clinicians in stressful hospital situations is provided in Coombs and Goldman (1973). This research, part of the larger study of medical socialization, was based upon participant observation in an intensive care unit.

7. Kasper (1959) first emphasized that medical students are desensitized not to death, but to the symbols of death.

8. For further discussion on this and other aspects of the desensitizing experience, see Lief and Fox's (1963) article.

9. Humor is also utilized as a tension release in subsequent stages of professional development. Lightheartedness in the midst of painful human drama might seem inappropriate, but it helps to reduce the emotional tension and strain created by stressful circumstances and thereby allows clinicians to perform their responsibilities more effectively.

10. The whole tone of the autopsy room differs from the clinical cadaver setting. There is only one body (instead of several lined up in rows), and it has not been chemically treated in any way as have the cadavers, so it is much easier to perceive it as a live person. Also, the attending physican is nearly always present (rather than anatomy instructors), and this helps define the dead person as a patient rather than a specimen.

11. Students rarely have an opportunity to follow a patient longitudinally, since their clinical assignments include frequent rotations from one clinical service to another. This shuttling back and forth from one hospital setting to another usually does not allow them enough time to form close personal attachments with patients.

12. For further reading on the social organization related to death in the hospital setting, see Sudnow (1967).

13. By the term "medical model," we mean primarily that system of clinical practice which exists in American teaching hospitals, one which includes a technological emphasis tending to exclude the humanistic dimensions of medical practice.

14. It is our impression that most clinicians who reach this questioning stage do so after graduating from medical school. But some clinical medical students are aware of the critical views of more advanced physicians. "I've heard that no one dies with dignity in this hospital," one said. "There is always a crowd of people around frantically working over him and hooking him up to gadgets."

15. In this regard, Mace (1971) has said, "If I may coin a word, I would suggest that the medical disease of today is 'pedestalitis.' The doctor is on a pedestal, and his elevation is to some extent gratifying; but it also makes him feel isolated, cut off, and somewhat insecure. . . . More and more he is seen as an authority figure, a busy human dynamo, who is not to be bothered with little human concerns and does not have time to sit down and talk. He is remote and detached, like the man who sits at the controls in the lonely box that operates a giant crane."

16. Technical jargon also helps avoid the stressful dialogue with patients and their families. These terms tend to isolate death by classifying it as a medical event—an event occurring in professional life rather than personal life. For further discussion about language as a coping mechanism, see Coombs and Goldman (1973).

17. There is evidence, too, that patients sometimes help doctors avoid the discomfort of talking about death by not asking questions or pressing for details. This reinforces the commonly held assumption that terminal patients do not want to talk about death.

18. Of course, those who become general practitioners avoid the residency stage. Also, internship has been eliminated in the training of some specialties.

19. For an interesting essay on the doctor and his training, see chapter 2, "The Man Behind the Stethoscope," in Greenberg (1965).

20. Glaser and Strauss (1968) have said, "The psychological aspects of dealing with the dying and their families are virtually absent from training. Hence, although physicians and nurses are highly skilled at handling the bodies of terminal patients, their behavior to them otherwise is actually outside the province of professional standards."

21. In other words, Stage V could come earlier and with much greater ease if medical educators would recognize and openly discuss with trainees their feelings about death and dying.

22. Recognizing this unmet human need, commercial agencies have sprung up to provide, for a fee, companions for those dying of incurable diseases. According to a UPI dispatch (Star Free Press, Ventura, California, February 27, 1975), this new service appears to be a lucrative business.

23. Kübler-Ross (1969) maintains that ours is the most death-denying society of all time. Because death has traditionally been a taboo subject, relatively little has

been written on the topic. Quite recently, however, an increasing number of books and articles have been written and seminars initiated on the new subject—"Thanatology, the study of death"—in colleges and medical schools.

24. We suspect, however, that there will be significant changes in the coming years. Research by Kübler-Ross and others has piqued interest and awareness of the problem. Most interesting are the developments of health-care organizations, like the New Haven Hospices, which furnish doctors and paramedics to monitor the dying patient and look after his welfare, counsel the family, and provide emotional support (Dobihal, 1974).

# REFERENCES

BLOOM, S. W. (1971) "The medical center as a social system," pp. 429-448 in R. H. Coombs and C. E. Vincent (eds.) Psychosocial Aspects of Medical Training. Springfield, Ill.: Charles C Thomas.

COOMBS, R. H. and L. J. GOLDMAN (1973) "Maintenance and discontinuity of coping mechanisms in an intensive-care unit." Social Problems 20 (Winter): 342-355.

DOBIHAL, E. F., Jr. (1974) "Talk on terminal care." Connecticut Medicine 38 (July): 364-367.

GLASER, B. G. and A. L. STRAUSS (1968) A Time for Dying. Chicago: Aldine.

GOUGH, H. G. and W. B. HALL (1975) "An attempt to predict graduation from medical school." J. of Medical Education 50 (October): 940-950.

GREENBERG, S. (1965) The Troubled Calling: Crisis in the Medical Establishment. New York: Macmillan.

KASPER, A. M. (1959) "The doctor and death," pp. 259-271 in H. Feifel (ed.) The Meaning of Death. New York: McGraw-Hill.

KUBLER-ROSS, E. (1969) On Death and Dying. New York: Macmillan.

LIEF, H. I. and R. C. FOX (1963) "The medical student's training for 'detached concern,'" pp. 12-35 in H. I. Lief, V. Lief and N. R. Lief (eds.) The Psychological Basis of Medical Practice. New York: Harper & Row.

LIFTON, R. J. and E. OLSON (1974) Living and Dying. New York: Praeger.

MACE, D. R. (1971) "Communication, interviewing, and the physician-patient relationship," pp. 380-403 in R. H. Coombs and C. E. Vincent (eds.) Psychosocial Aspects of Medical Training. Springfield, Ill.: Charles C Thomas.

MERTON, R. K. (1957) "Some preliminaries to a sociology of medical education," pp. 3-79 in R. K. Merton, G. Reader and P. L. Kendall (eds.) The Student-Physician: Introductory Studies in the Sociology of Medical Education. Cambridge, Mass.: Harvard Univ. Press.

PARSONS, T. and V. LIDZ (1967) "Death in American society," pp. 133-170 in E. S. Shneidman (ed.) Essays in Self-Destruction. New York: Science House.

SUDNOW, D. (1967) Passing On: The Social Organization of Dying. Englewood Cliffs, N.J.: Prentice-Hall.

JOHN LOFLAND, Professor of Sociology, University of California, Davis and founding editor of *Urban Life,* is currently completing a treatise titled *Interaction Strategies.* His previous works include *Doomsday Cult, Deviance and Identity,* and *Analyzing Social Settings.*

# OPEN AND CONCEALED DRAMATURGIC STRATEGIES:

## The Case of the State Execution

### JOHN LOFLAND

SOCIAL ORGANIZATIONS VARY in the degree to which their copings with basic aspects of life and death are dramaturgically open or concealed. A concealed dramaturgics of life and death events erects physical, social, and psychological barriers to perception, regulates the entrance and exit of participants and witnesses, controls publicity, and minimizes temporal duration, among other things. An open dramaturgics allows and even promotes the opposite.

One way usefully to conceive that enormous transformation in the western world typically captioned, "the industrial revolution," is as a shift from open to concealed dramaturgics in the management of many life and death matters. The primal scenes of fornicating, birthing, wedding, and dying (of humans *and* other animals) have shifted from relatively commonplace openness to delicate concealment. The historically open and ubiquitous acts of defecation and urination and their products have become shielded and contained. Disease, hunger, gross

AUTHOR'S NOTE: I am indebted to Katherine Buckles for library search assistance.

impairment and deformity of the body have been metaphorically and literally swept out of the streets and held behind walls. Disputes historically managed with the directness of violence, duels, and other open contests have become mediated, elaborate, convoluted, and conspiratorial affairs.

Taking this asserted dramaturgical revolution as our context, I want here to analyze how one life and death event has been dramaturgically transformed from historic to modern times. That event is the *state execution.* Its *invariant* features are the space-time specific scene of a court sentencing a person to die; from there and then in court that person must—by some means, someplace, by someone—be killed. How is this to be accomplished? How open or concealed are people to be about the invariant fact that a human being is going to die, is dying, and is now dead?

This question needs to be addressed at two levels, the ideal-typical (or logical) and the historical-empirical. Irrespective of how any society has *actually* managed the matter of state executions, of what practices would each, *logically,* consist? What are features of an ideally concealed and ideally open state execution? The ideal-typical profiles to be presented provide guides, as it were, in terms of which actual, concrete state executions can be judged for the degree of their openness or concealment. At the historical-empirical level, the state executions of England and the United States (and to some extent all of Europe and the world) in the 1600s and 1700s, as contrasted with state executions in those countries in the 1900s, seem, at least in composite, remarkably to approximate the ideal-typical profiles. Within the confines of severe space limitations, I will try to provide sufficient empirical material to lend at least some credibility to this assertion of enormously opposed dramaturgic strategies.[1]

By way of overview, eleven phases (or at least aspects) are employed in explicating the ideal types and in contrasting "historic" (circa 1700) and "modern" (circa 1950) state executions in England and America: the death wait, death confinement, execution time, death trip, death place, death witnesses, executioners, features of the condemned him- or herself, technique of death, corpse disposal, and death announcement.

## THE DEATH WAIT

In a concealed dramaturgics, the time between sentencing and execution is kept as short as possible. The longer the condemned is left alive, the more the act of execution can be thought about, and can be an embarrassment. Ideally, the condemned is executed immediately.

Ironically, this initial point of contrast is opposite to dramaturgic expectations. However open historic executions were in other regards, they missed the boat here, so to speak, by (especially in the 1600s and earlier) often taking the condemned directly from trial to execution. English law of 1752 required that murderers be hanged on the day after sentencing; by the 1820s many capital offenders were "tried on a Friday and executed in rows of from three to six the following Monday" (Laurence, 1960: 102). Such dispatch obviously limits the degree to which the reality of the death can be communicated, a deficiency for which, as we shall see however, historic executions more than compensated.

Modern executions have tended to enormously longer death waits, averaging a year or two at various periods in England and the United States (United Nations, 1968). In some cases, death waits have gone on for a decade. It is the stern reality that such waits display that seem, indeed, to generate so much strong feeling about state executions, as among those who argue that long waits (caused, proximately, by the availability and use of appellate and executive remedies) are "cruel and unusual punishment."

## DEATH CONFINEMENT

If there is to be much time between sentencing and execution, the condemned must be kept someplace. If the presence of the now "living dead" is to be minimized, he needs to be kept sequestered in a concealed place, visitor access to which is either prohibited or minimized under stringent regulations. Obviously, the more people who interact with the condemned, the more that can be reported, thought, and perhaps even done about him.

Historic death confinements—prisons—were much more bustling, lively, and emotionally polymorphic places than their austere and solemn modern counterparts. Before middle-class prissiness and universalistic bureaucrats took over the management of prisons, the more colorful and wealthy of condemned persons, at least, could enjoy the companionship of virtually any visitors they desired. Popular criminals were visited by "men and women of the highest position." Perhaps the most famous, Jack Sheppard, executed in 1724, received "no fewer than three thousand persons" in his death cell in Newgate Prison (Bleackley, 1975: 79). In 1744, another had "seven girls to dine with him on the evening before he was hanged...," a party at which the condemned was reported "not less cheerful than those who hoped to live longer" (Atholl, 1954: 66). Alcohol and other amenities were available, prompting some contemporaries to complain that their effects detracted from an appropriate pale of death.

It was, indeed, against these kinds of easy and open death confinements that such champions of austerity as William Fielding and Charles Dickens railed. Dickens in 1849 plotted out the concealed strategy of state executions that was to become the reigning reality of virtually the entire world within a hundred years.

> From the moment of a murderer's being sentenced to death, I would dismiss him to . . . dread obscurity. . . . I would allow no curious visitors to hold any communication with him; I would place every

obstacle in the way of his sayings and doings being served up in print on Sunday mornings for the perusal of families. . . .

We should not return to the days when ladies paid visits to highwaymen, drinking their punch in the condemned cells of Newgate [Dickens, 1892: 242, 243].

Modern dramaturgy is, nonetheless, a bit less strict, "the prevailing [world-wide] practice is to keep condemned prisoners in solitary confinement and under heavy surveillance, but to allow them special privileges" (United Nations, 1968: 99). Among these privileges is, in some jurisdictions, access to sedative drugs, the better to inhibit any disconcerting breakdowns.

To be open about death is, in part, to talk about it, to impress upon the condemned the imminence of his own demise. Historic executions had *death talk specialists,* people whose duty it was forcefully to impress the condemned with their state. By forcefully, I mean that the condemned was required to listen to them and that their actions were vigorously performed. The sexton of St. Sepulchre's church fulfilled such a role on the eve of executions in London. He came tolling a handbell under the windows of Newgate Prison, chanting verses recommending repentance. Given the high frequency of executions, he was a familiar sight and sound. Prison clergymen were even more ubiquitous and formidable figures. At Newgate, the condemned sat in the Condemned Pew of the prison's chapel and suffered admonitions during the compulsory and daily religious service attended by all prisoners. The condemned were also often subjected to a special religious service close to the time of execution. In one version, all condemned sat round a coffin listening to a sermon, perhaps hearing the ceremony for the burial of the dead. In another version, the last service and sermon on torments the condemned could expect to suffer after death were so harrowing and upsetting that they became a popular entertainment for the aristocratic ladies and gentlemen of London. Sheriffs sometimes had to control attendance by ticket. The clergy of Newgate, especially, seemed to enjoy their work, for complaints of over-zealousness were sometimes lodged, and authorities on one occasion censured an Ordinary for "harrowing a prisoner's feelings unnecessarily" (Bleackley, 1975: 262). The contrast with the modern concealed strategy is striking: such specialists today are mild-mannered and their employment is optional.[2]

## DEATH TIME

In a concealed dramaturgics, the execution is most auspiciously scheduled on a day of the week and at a time of the day that is socially inconspicuous. The day ought not meaningfully to coincide with the society's sacred days, be these religious or frivolous. An inconspicuous hour of the chosen day likewise deemphasizes the event.

Historic British executions occurred (in public) in the early afternoon, insuring the largest number of possible witnesses. But modern executions, despite the shield of a physically enclosed place, tend to concealed times: early morning (such as 7 or 8 o'clock) or late at night (such as 11 o'clock). The prison context has frequently prompted officials to choose times when prisoners are locked in their cells or fully at their work. A prison population at milling leisure is a population thought too easily preoccupied with the execution—hence, the marginal execution times (Atholl, 1954: 41).

## THE DEATH TRIP

The condemned must in some manner be removed from the death cell and taken to the death place. A dramaturgics of openness—of bluntly proclaiming the condemned's imminent death—is a dramaturgics in which the trip itself is long, accomplished by elaborate transport devices, employs a complicated cortege, enjoys dramatic events along the way, traverses a complex and public route, and promotes long and complex talk along the route and at the execution. Such were the drama-turgics of historic death trips.

(a) In early years, executions were often held on the spot of the condemned's crime, a feature making for long death trips from the prison. In London, as in other cities, particular spots came to be places of public execution. The use of Tyburn, a site more than two miles through crowded streets from Newgate prison—the place of the condemned—necessitated the ideal-type of open dramaturgic routing. While the route was less than three miles long, it sometimes required up to three hours to move the condemned this distance. The modern concealed strategy, in contrast, brings the condemned within a few steps of the death place beforehand (while not letting him perceive it). The British have even devoted considerable study to shortening the distance and timing the interval between calling upon the condemned in his cell and actually killing him. In some places, it was reduced to "eight steps" and in the range of nine to fifteen seconds (Scott, 1950: 209-210). Pinioning devices of lightning applica-tion and drills in cap and rope placement insure that the walk and the hanging happen so fast that one need watch closely in order to see it—to know that it in fact happened. (British gallows redesign of 1876 provided a scaffold-top lever for releasing the drop, thus eliminating the delay between adjusting the noose, descending the steps and going under the scaffold to draw the bolt.) Electrocution death trips are reported to be a bit slower, requiring somewhat more than a minute fully to accomplish (Elliott, 1940: 144).

(b) Eight steps and fifteen seconds contrast with the dramatic, historic flair of earlier times when the condemned were transported on hurdles or in horse-drawn carts along with their coffins. More wealthy or popular condemned were allowed to ride in mourning coaches. Thus elevated, condemned were visible to crowds of spectators who lined the route, or who merely happened to see them while conducting their routine pursuits in the action-filled streets of preindustrial cities (L. Lofland, 1973: ch. 2).

(c) Condemned were taken quite seriously in the sense that they were the stars of a cortege of several hundred people, which was typically "headed by the city marshal on horseback, followed by the undersheriff with a cavalcade of peace officers, and a body of constables armed with staves. Then came the cart or carts with the condemned, more constables, and finally a company of javelin men. Sometimes a party of javelin men headed the procession" (Laurence, 1960: 187). When the condemned were markedly popular or unpopular, there might be more armed strength, the better to protect against the mob's rescuing or killing them. Cutting the trip to a few steps and seconds drastically reduces the possibilities of forming a cortege which in modern times amounts to a mere four or five career officials, or even less when the trip is very short.

(d) Historic London corteges passed through narrow, people-glutted streets in which spectators pressed upon the procession. Popular condemned were cheered and kisses were blown at them; despised condemned were jeered, hissed, groaned at and pelted with garbage and mud. The scene was frequently one of confusion and borderline chaos, a scene in sharp contrast to the modern, de-peopled, streamlined death trip.

(e) As befits a social event, the cortege made stops; its course was punctuated by *events* which more clearly indicated the kind of procession afoot. These included a church stop, pub stops, and friend stops (Mencken, 1942). *Running conversations* took place between the condemned in the cart and his friends who walked or rode part of the distance with him (Bleackley, 1933: 50; Laurence, 1960: 66). Fifteen seconds and eight steps allow for none of this.

(f) The jiggling of the cart, its various stops and starts, mountings and dismountings, and flying objects made for an obstacle-ridden course. Upon arriving at the death place, the condemned perhaps had even to climb a ladder or mount steps, depending upon the technique of the time. The condemned, that is, very much *interacted with his situation,* thereby expressing himself in calmness, clumsiness, or whatever. Modern executions prevent such expression by abbreviating the death walk, the ultimate abbreviation being the construction of the death cell and chamber on the identical level so that the condemned will not encounter grades.[3]

(g) Last, throughout the death trip there was a torrent of words: from the mob in the street; between the condemned and their friends and others; between officials and the crowd; from the clergy who orated at various points; and from the condemned in his death speech. Throughout, moreover, church bells tolled. Modern death trips are virtually wordless and no bells toll.

Thus, historic death trips were dramaturgically open: long in time and distance, complex in transport, large and heterogeneous in cortege and spectators, complex and diverse in events and routing, and long and complicated in verbal interaction.

## DEATH PLACE

Social places vary in the degree to which they are dramaturgically open or concealed. Dramaturgically open places provide unobstructed views of contained activities, of "front" and "back" regions.[4] Dramaturgically concealed places obstruct viewing by (1) erecting physical barriers, and (2) guiding and controlling what the viewer sees despite physical barriers.

Historic state executions were ideal-typically open. They took place outdoors, in early periods, in open fields and later in city streets. Even when made closed to the public, they remained outdoors for a time, in prison yards. Their "roof" was the sky, their "walls" the horizon or exteriors of buildings. Death was in this sense "integrated" with much else in social life. Modern executions, in contrast, are extremely concealed within doors, often even in windowless rooms.

Early historic executions were highly integrated in the additional sense that they took place at the scene of the condemned's crime—that is, in multiple and unspecialized places. Over time, certain places specialized in executions, as at the famous Tyburn, but there were many such local places.

Modern societies have moved decisively to concealment by having only one place of execution for large regions or for the entire society. These are called execution "chambers" or "sheds," terms tellingly revealing their concealed character. The movement is, in one sense, from a highly personalized to a highly impersonalized place; from an open definition of the condemned's personal identity at the place of his particular crime to an obscured and generalized treatment of him at a centralized place where everybody and anybody and hence "nobody" is executed.[5] Even the exteriors of modern death places are highly inaccessible to view in that they are always inside prison walls.

## DEATH WITNESSES

Historic executions attracted many by-standing witnesses, and were indeed held in the public outdoors partly for that reason. Hundreds and even thousands of persons appeared. The most famous or infamous condemned could draw enormous crowds (50-100,000 or more, according to some estimates). A hanging on New York's Bedloe's Island in 1860 had "steam-boats, barges, oyster sloops, yachts and rowboats swarm[ing] everywhere in view of the gallows. Large steamers such as carry hundreds of people . . . on pleasure excursions were there, so laden with a living freight of curious people that it seemed almost a wonder that they did not sink. There were barges . . . with awnings spread, under which those who were thirsty imbibed lager beer" (eyewitness account reprinted in Mencken, 1942: 175). Sometimes people packed city streets so tightly that fear and panic ensued, killing a few and injuring dozens.[6]

These many witnesses were extremely *diverse* in social standing and types of social identity. First, most infamous and most numerous were what is variously called the rabble, the mob and the dregs. This was itself a heterogeneous assortment of pickpockets, harlots, unemployed, highwaymen, rogues, dandies, floaters, trollops, ruffians, thieves, vagabonds, and criminals, to use a few terms of contemporary observers. Second, hawkers circulated selling broadsides detailing the life, crimes and words of the condemned, and foods such as sweetmeats, tarts, meatpies and oranges. Third, children were brought by schoolmasters and mothers to be morally instructed and edified. To warn a child he might come to a bad end had literal meaning in the rope he saw directly. Fourth, in favored places arranged by the sheriff and in discreetly rented windows, various aristocrats watched. Fifth, many businesses closed so their owners, craftsmen and tradesmen, and their families might enjoy the "hanging day." Sixth, soldiers, constables, and other agents of state force strove to prevent the crowd from pressing too close upon the gallows and to keep order generally. Larger executions employed several hundred agents of state force. Seventh and last, intellectuals and reporters were present, some to enjoy and some to deplore the execution horrors in their subsequent writings. Boswell is among the most famous of the enthusiastic regulars at hangings, while William Makepeace Thackeray (1968) and Charles Dickens were repulsed by them.

If these are some of the main classes of witnesses, what were they *doing* before, during and after the execution? First and most striking, many were engaged in a complex of acts best labeled holiday-making, consisting of sporadic group singing, food munching, joking, shouting, beverage sipping, and the like. The mood was as at a "sporting occasion" or fair. Rough play and fights punctuated time in encounters of pushing, tripping, "kicking dirt about," wrestling and straight fighting over imagined or real offenses. The press of the crowd and excitement caused faintings among the "gentler sex" who were often "indecently exposed" in the course of being taken away. Pickpocketing and pickups were rampant. Occasionally, large, packed-in crowds panicked, trampling and killing many of their number. Agents of state force—be they gaolers, constables, soldiers or police—worked at order-keeping, arresting thieves, striking spectators to keep them back from the procession or the gallows, fighting off attacks on the condemned, the executioner, or both, and so forth. However, a large proportion of the witnesses simply engaged in quiet socializing while waiting, perhaps discussing other executions of their acquaintance or other matters of the day. When the scaffold or the condemned arrived at the appointed time, crowd acknowledgments went up. Witnesses continued to yell comments during the execution itself. If the condemned were faced away from the crowd, or people could not see, shouts of "turn him around," and "stand out of the way" were forthcoming. Despised criminals were likely to hang to the accompaniment of yelling and shouting. Witnesses were sometimes direct participants, as when they rescued the condemned, or carried him off for resuscitation after hanging. Friends of the condemned were sometimes allowed to pull his legs after he was suspended in order to shorten the agony of strangulation. Last, but far from least, businessmen and intellectuals of the bourgeoisie were deploring it all.

The dramaturgic openness of (a) large numbers of witnesses, (b) wearing diverse social identities, and (c) carrying on heterogeneous activities in the historic era contrasts sharply with the concealed character of (a) a small number of witnesses, (b) wearing a narrow range of social identities, and (c) engaging in a homogeneous set of activities in the modern era.

Virtually throughout the world, executions are, as reported in a United Nations survey, "not held in public view and attendance is carefully limited and controlled" (United Nations, 1968: 103). Execution "chambers" themselves limit the possible number—holding 50 to 75 people if they are packed in—and statutes often specify maximums, as in the United States in the nineteen sixties where the number varied from three to twenty (United Nations, 1968: 103).

Witnesses are sometimes excluded altogether, allowing only executional personnel per se. When permitted, they are defined as "symbolic representatives" of the public at large and typically include newspaper reporters, representatives of the prosecution, defense, or both, and perhaps members of the condemned's family. The presence of others may be left to the discretion of the prison wardens, who, it seems, have tended to prefer politicians, other government officials, and professionals such as doctors from among the thousands who make application to be witnesses (e.g. Elliott, 1940: 230-233). Following the British, "the trend in most countries now is increasingly to exclude [journalists] from attendance," or to set strict limits and rules on what and how they report (United Nations, 1968: 103-104).

Witnesses and executioners alike hardly say or do anything, owing in part to the short period of time available to them. A large sign reading "SILENCE" hanging over the door into the Sing Sing death chamber epitomizes the modern stance and reduces witnesses to conversing in "low voices" while waiting, if they talk at all (Elliott, 1940: 142). Even photography is specifically forbidden.

Overall, then, the modern dramaturgy of concealment—of virtual denial—is impressive: there are, at most, a handful of silent, carefully selected, and constrained witnesses.

## EXECUTIONERS

Like the witnesses before whom they performed, historic executioners were a colorful, robust, and rule-breaking lot—in their personal lives as well as in their roles as executioners. They comported themselves in ways that endowed them with distinctive public and personal identities; they performed their duties along lines of their personal choosing and they related to the condemned in a personal manner. Modern executioners, in contrast, are virtually anonymous, bland, and colorless men who carry out bureaucratically generated and well-practiced "drills" upon the condemned, who are treated in a severely impersonal manner. The historic executioner dealt honestly and directly with death; the modern one bounds flinchingly by it.

(a) Historic public executions rendered executioners public figures. As the ultimate and personally-known agents of state force, they attracted much interest, both supportive and threatening. They were ostracized or lionized depending upon whom, and from what social group, they had most recently executed. Either way, they were "celebrities" about whom stories circulated and comment was made. As is inherent in being somebody, there was imputed to them stereotyped personal characters. Horace Bleackley (1975) has chronicled this nicely for historic London hangmen, as in brutal Price (1714-1715), grim Marvell (1715-1717), laughing Hooper (1728-1735), morose Botting (1817-1820), indifferent Calcraft (1829-1874), and gentleman Marwood (1874-1883). Each was endowed with a unique, distinctive, and public personality; each had a personal style. Flattered or insulted, each *existed.*

They existed, in part, because being an executioner was a full-time job. Business was heavy and social ostracism was strong; they were barred from other modes of employment even when they wanted to quit. Moreover, their "deviances" did not get them fired. When executions moved indoors and became private, executioners gradually ceased to be publicly known figures and, moreover, the volume of executions decreased. Executioner is a part-time job in the modern era. As a consequence, executioners have become virtual non-entities.[7]

(b) Historic executions, being less routinized and specified, facilitated the expression of personal character. At an execution in 1760 "the sheriffs fell to eating and drinking on the scaffold and helped up one of their friends to drink with them as [the condemned] was still hanging" (eyewitness account reprinted in Mencken, 1942: 240). London's hangman of 45 years, William Calcraft, joked and swore at executions, wearing, indeed, a rose in his buttonhole. Thomas Cheshire, who practiced between 1808 and 1840, openly relished his work, as described by one eyewitness (Bleackley, 1975: 196-197), pouncing upon the condemned with a "basilisk gleam" in his eye and a "stealthy cat-like clutch." Many liked their duties less and performed them drunk; one was so intoxicated he had to be restrained from hanging the clergyman by mistake (Atholl, 1954: 143).

Detailed, technical aspects of executions were left to the executioner, thus allowing for "mistakes." Some bought cheap rope that broke; others were "incompetent even in the tying of knots." Occasionally, the executioner and other officials fell to arguing upon the scaffold over the adjustment of the rope, the length of the drop, or the division of the condemned's property (Atholl, 1954: 143; Bleackley, 1975: 128, 181).

The incredible quickness of the modern execution largely robs executioners of opportunities for self-expression. Like much modern work, individual variation and craftsmanship have been engineered out. Those involved in the modern British execution even called it "the drill" and practiced hangings with a dummy. The "engineering out" occurred historically among the British through a set of parliamentary commissions that studied the subject "scientifically" and produced a collective, binding set of procedures. Individual craft was thus transformed into bureaucratic procedure. While historic executioners supplied some equipment (for example, rope, pinioning harness), modern ones have everything carefully supplied and controlled by the state.

Procedural rationalization requires, of course, methodical and objective recruitment of personnel (including technical testing and character assessment) and formal training. Both procedures have been undertaken for modern British and other executioners.[8] This is a far cry from the historic practice of haphazard recruiting and "training" among the condemned and the kinsmen and friends of executioners.

(c) Modern executions severely restrict and impersonalize the duration and amount of contact between executioner and condemned. No or few words need pass between them. There is virtually no bodily contact or other vehicle of personalism, such as the passing of goods or money. The executioner need never even see the condemned except during the few seconds of the execution. Accompanying prison officers may purposively be strangers to the condemned, the better to inhibit the emotional arousal of all parties (see Elliott, 1940: 130; Atholl, 1954: 133). All these narrowings of the relation serve the purpose of death concealment.

Historic executions had much more *talking and viewing* between executioner and condemned. Executioners might visit the condemned in order to console or admonish (in addition to sizing up for the drop). Hangmen customarily requested and received the condemneds' pardon for executing them. In England, the condemned gave the executioner cash, presents and his clothes. Because execution techniques were uncertain in their effectiveness, the executioner was tipped in cash or expensive objects, such as a watch, in the hope of improved service. Such gifts might be openly awarded upon the gallows. Additional money was realized from the sale of the con-demned's clothes which the executioner was likely to strip from the corpse at the scene, just before placing it in the coffin. The hanging rope was often cut up into short lengths and sold. The stripping of clothes involved, of course, the personalism and intimacy of physical contact, as did the standard practice of pulling the condemned's legs as he hung, the quicker to bring death.

In such ways as these, the historic executioner and his condemned experienced a direct and personal relation to each other. In all these ways, the executioners dealt openly with the fact that someone was dying.


## CONDEMNED

We have seen that historic death cells and trips, especially, provided the condemned with a margin of freedom to express their personal uniqueness. They were visited and went visiting; they were talked to and talked. This leeway to behave in diverse and personal ways facilitated others' perceiving them as particular and unique humans. Death was thus personalized and, in this sense, dramaturgically open, as opposed to the dramaturgic concealment and impersonalization of masking and suppressing diverse personal expressions. Historic executions continued this leeway through the execution itself in permitted accouterments, actions and words.

(a) Condemned of substance and flair were allowed to express these qualities. Aristocrats and dandy highwaymen decked themselves in formal finery, perhaps in the manner of the Earl of Essex who, in 1600, wore "a gown of wrought velvet, a satin suit, and a felt hat, all of black, and with a small ruff about his neck" (Laurence, 1960: 125). Peculiarities of taste, such as wearing a wedding suit or a shroud, were permitted. One wealthy condemned rode to Tyburn in his own mourning carriage drawn by six horses. More modest bits of executional equipment might be supplied by the condemned: cushions or handkerchiefs on which to kneel and pray upon the scaffold; a pliable silken rather than stiff hemp rope in order to hasten strangulation; black handerkerchiefs with which to be blindfolded, bound at the wrists, or drop as a signal to execute; presents for the executioners.

(b) The final moments of the execution scene were not hurried through in wordless, rushed fashion as is the modern penchant. Their public character seemed, indeed, to have encouraged the condemned to give vent to an array of rather histrionic actions and words. Friends and acquaintances might be acknowledged and greeted. A condemned's infant child or others might be kissed or otherwise given farewell gestures. Deep formal bows might be directed to the crowd. An orange might be sucked upon, a pinch of snuff taken, or other minor comforts indulged in. Possessions and money might be presented as gifts to officials or nearby friends. Those who disliked the clergy's readings, prayers, and demands for repentance might counter with pithy putdowns as in shouting, "There is no God, or if there is, I hold him in defiance" (Atholl, 1954: 62). Contempt might be expressed by kicking one's shoes into the crowd (thus depriving the executioner of one of his perquisites) or by doing a dance. Ineffective pinioning methods made struggling defiance possible through wrestling, striking, or kicking the executioners. In one hanging, the condemned three times hauled himself up and straddled the trap door, finally necessitating three men to hold him at rope's end. More compliant condemned gave *help* to their executioners, perhaps by kissing the rope, positioning the noose, shaking hands and formally forgiving them, or dropping or waving a handkerchief when ready. Most spectacularly, condemned might deliver long and elaborately prepared scaffold speeches. Last-minute reprieves were not uncommon in the historic era, a fact that encouraged "long discourses and prayers," perhaps "lamenting misdeeds," expounding "pious sentiments" and exhorting the crowd to avoid crime.

Taken together, the condemned had abundant opportunities to establish for themselves a *public character,* be that character heroic, villainous, courageous, cowardly, or whatever, and this possibility was founded upon the loose and uncodified conduct of executions and their public setting. Historic condemned were permitted, that is, to *personalize* the scene through showing the capacity for personal taste and preference and through speaking and acting. In this sense, the fact that a person was dying was openly communicated.

Modern executions, in contrast, prohibit this array of character-endowing possibilities—visiting, pub-stopping, speech-making, resistance, and the like. Not least of blandness-producing strategies is the engineering of swiftness: it is obviously hard to *be* anybody in but nine, fifteen, or sixty seconds. Even when a few "last words" are allowed (and not all modern executions allow any), the process moves in a manner so mechanized that it doubtless serves to inhibit speaking by many condemned. As hangman Berry would say to condemned upon entering the death hold: "If you have anything to say, now is the time, because once I get you on the scaffold you won't have time" (Atholl, 1954: 139). Referring to the 387 electrocutions he performed, Robert Elliott (1940: 66-67) describes the condemned as behaving virtually without exception as "meek as lambs." That is a way to go, of course, but it is only one of many historic ways. As one commentator has put it about England, "the old legends of courage on the scaffold . . . would not have sprung from executions as practiced . . . [there]" in modern times (Maddox, 1969: 87). Nor are other character styles very possible, such as the sniveling coward, the defiant sociopath, the eloquent revolutionary, the indifferent retardate or the dazed ordinary bloke. Such practices as state-controlled or provided clothes and brisk, machine-like treatment from approach in the death cell through a short death march thus serve well to *impersonalize* and to conceal.

## DEATH TECHNIQUE

The condemned must by some technique be killed. How, dramaturgically, is this to be accomplished? A strategy of dramaturgic openness makes inescapably clear the existential fact that a human being is being killed. How is this done? The technique should be highly unreliable and ineffective, take a long time to work, make a great deal of noise, mutilate the body and inflict terrible pain, causing the condemned to cry out in anguish and struggle strongly to resist—all of which actions are highly visible to witnesses and accompanied by noxious and abundant odors. Not all historic executions could claim to display all these features of openness, but, on the whole, they were rather well approximated. The modern concealed strategy of killing while looking the other way, so to speak, strives to achieve the opposite: unfailing, lightning fast, noiseless technique that is painless and nonmutilating, involves no struggle, dying sounds, or odors, and is carried out in a way that shields the condemned's body in case something "goes wrong" despite all precautions. Modern people call this "humane." Dramaturgically, it is concealed.

Space prohibits examination of various techniques in these nine terms. It must suffice to say that such ancient and historic ones as pressing to death by progressively heavy weights upon the chest, breaking upon the wheel, crucifixion, stoning, strangling, burning at the stake, cutting off strips of flesh, stabbing non-vital parts of the body, throat slitting, drawing and quartering, garroting, beheading, and premodern (short-drop) hanging are all enormously more open than concealed in these dramaturgic regards.

The five, major techniques of modern times—long-drop hanging, electrocution, lethal chamber, firing squad, and guillotine—vie with one another in terms of how well each approximates the nine ideally concealed qualities. The firing squad and guillotine are markedly more noisy or mutilating than the others and appear to be losing ground for those reasons. Electrocutions apparently have some duration, noise, sound, and odor (flesh sizzling) problems, as does the lethal chamber with regard to contortions. Long-drop hanging as perfected and practiced by the British is most ideally concealed, but even it is not dramaturgically perfect. Indeed, the search for a technique that more fully operationalizes these nine principles still goes on among those moderns still executing or thinking about doing it. Before abolition of capital punishment in Britain, the lethal injection or tranquilizer was officially considered. At least one U.S. state governor has in recent times made the same suggestion.[9]

## CORPSE DISPOSAL

An open dramaturgics of corpse disposal occurs in (1) a public manner that is (2) reasonably prolonged and that (3) brings the corpse to rest in some obvious and marked place. A concealed dramaturgics disposes of the corpse in (1) a private manner carried out in (2) a brief period of time that (3) brings the corpse to rest in an obscure and unmarked place.

Historic folk had some ingenious devices for actualizing these principles of openness. The common British and European practice of gibbeting expresses them best, by far. However killed, the corpse was somewhat preserved by boiling or tarring and hung up in a chain or wicker "suit" at the scene of the crime, along heavily travelled roads and rivers, or at a special gibbet place. The preservative retarded decay, and the chain or wicker "suit" prevented large parts of the corpse from detaching. By such means, the corpse's public display was prolonged. Carrion birds eventually picked the bones clean. Less public, prolonged and marked, but reasonably so, is the historic English practice of anatomization or dissection. In its most extreme form, the corpse was conveyed through the crowded streets of London to the barber-surgeons for public display and dissection before an auditorium packed with spectators (who were sometimes charged admission).

The opposite principles were likewise well actualized in the modern British practice of holding an inquest in the prison just after the execution and thereupon burying the body in an unmarked, quicklimed grave within the prison walls. Execution and complete disposal were thus accomplished in but a few hours and within a small, protected space. Only a minimum of officially required personnel were involved.

## DEATH ANNOUNCEMENT

A state execution is "announced" to the degree that members of the society not present at it are aware of its occurrence and of its social and physical details. An open dramaturgics strives to maximize, and a concealed dramaturgics to minimize, the number of "absentees" who know and the amount of detail they possess.

Today the ideally open announcement would presumably involve something on the order of world-wide live television, repeated often on videotape, and embroidered by the observations of experts and other moralists (such as the Pope and Norman Mailer). Unrestrained print media would provide more permanent and weighty words and pictures. Announcements of historic executions were as open as technology then allowed. Newspaper, broadside and pamphlet accounts were produced in profusion. (Before the age of printing, the condemned's corpse was left to be its own announcement.) Historic folk employed, moreover, *symbolic acts* from which a modern dramaturgics of openness could well borrow: church bells were tolled, black flags were run up, public notices were posted. Many shops and schools were closed by their master's absence on a hanging day. In modern society the closing of government, educational and other establishments would have a similar announcing effect upon the citizenry.

A dramaturgics of "concealed" announcements is obvious. All publicizing media are barred; witnesses, who might talk, are few and controlled; government notice is zero. This was virtually the modern British practice, among whom executions were classified as official state secrets.


## CONCLUDING REMARKS

I have suggested two sharply different dramaturgic strategies of dealing with basic events of life and death and offered an idealized model of them for the specific event of the state execution. Materials on "historic" and "modern" state executions in England and America have been reviewed in terms of the degree to which they illustrate and approximate such open versus concealed dramaturgics.

If, as I asserted at the outset, the state execution is only one special front on which there has been a "dramaturgic revolution," then there is a need to specify carefully how and to what degree this has or has not occurred in other areas—most saliently, more routine dying, birth, and such on-going body functions as defecation, urination, and fornication. Among more "social" areas of life and death, open versus concealed stagings of hierarchical relations merit special attention.

As an application of the dramaturgical perspective, this analysis assumes that *how people do things, the style in which they do things, is virtually as important as what they do, the substance of their actions.* The world is ruled perhaps as much by the dramaturgic encasement of actions as by the actions encased. Public figures, especially, rise and fall as much on the manner they display as on the actions they perform. Of late, this realization has been elaborated into operating procedures of enormous efficiency, particularly in the creation and promotion of political figures. Relative to state executions, it may be suggested that they rise and fall as a function of how they are done and not merely because they are done. To the degree they persist, they do so by means of the concealment strategy explicated.

## NOTES

1. For topically and empirically expanded treatment, differently framed, see J. Lofland (1975).

2. See, further, J. Lofland (1975) on insulation of the death cell from noises of the death preparations.

3. Scott, 1950: 209. In one innovation, the rope is held daintily off the scaffold floor by a silk cord, the better to insure the condemned will not trip.

4. On this and other concepts of the dramaturgic perspective, see Goffman (1959).

5. The larger the number of places and the greater the number of people proximate to them, the greater, presumably, the likelihood of thinking about what happens in them.

6. See, e.g., Bleackley, 1975: 142-143; Mencken, 1942: 170ff.; Atholl, 1954: 79-80.

7. Cf. Hornum (1968). Sources of personal diversity of executioners in their deviances, misfortunes and "personalities" are discussed in J. Lofland (1975).

8. Laurence (1960: 137) sums up modern British executioners as "quiet men and well behaved." These formalizations are interestingly satirized in Duff (1955).

9. Sacramento Bee (1973). For extended discussion of the comparative dramaturgic characteristics of various death techniques, see J. Lofland (1975); see also Schmidt (1928) and Earle (1969).

## REFERENCES

ATHOLL, J. (1954) Shadow of the Gallows. London: John Long.

BLEACKLEY, H. (1975) The Hangmen of England. Montclair, N.J.: Patterson Smith. (originally published 1929)

——— (1933) Jack Sheppard. London: William Hodge and Company Ltd.

DICKENS, C. (1892) "Letters to the Editor of the London Times, November 13, November 17, 1849," pp. 241-244 in Vol. 22, The Works of Charles Dickens (National Library ed.). New York: Bigelow, Brown.

DUFF, C. (1955) A Handbook on Hanging: Finally Revised Edition. London: Putnam.

EARLE, A. M. (1969) Curious Punishments of Bygone Days. Montclair, N.J.: Patterson Smith. (originally published 1896)

ELLIOTT, R. C. (1940) Agent of Death: Memoirs of an Executioner. New York: E. P. Dutton.

GOFFMAN, E. (1959) The Presentation of Self in Everyday Life. Garden City, N.Y.: Doubleday-Anchor.

HORNUM, F. (1968) "The executioner." in M. Truzzi (ed.) Sociology and Everyday Life. Englewood Cliffs, N.J.: Prentice-Hall.

LAURENCE, J. (1960) A History of Capital Punishment. New York: Citadel Press.

LOFLAND, J. (1975) "The dramaturgics of state executions," introduction to Horace Bleackley, The Hangmen of England. Montclair, N.J.: Patterson Smith.

LOFLAND, L. H. (1973) A World of Strangers: Order and Action in Urban Public Space. New York: Basic Books.

MADDOX, J. (1969) "An indecent ritual," in Louis Blom-Cooper (ed.) The Hanging Question. London: Gerald Duckworth.

MENCKEN, A. [ed.] (1942) By the Neck: A Book of Hangings. New York: Hastings House.

ROBIN, G. (1964) "The executioner: his place in English society." British J. of Sociology 15: 243-253.

Sacramento Bee (1973) "Reagan's humane death penalty raises serious questions of ethics." September 29: 1.

SCHMIDT, F. (1928) "A Hangman's Diary: Being the Journal of Master Franz Schmidt Public Executioner of Nuremberg, 1573-1617. London: Philip Allan.

SCOTT, G. R. (1950) The History of Capital Punishment. London: Torchstream.

THACKERAY, W. M. (1968) "Going to see a man hanged," pp. 417-431 in Vol. 26, The Works of William Makepeace Thackeray. New York: AMS Press. (reprinted from Fraser's Magazine, August 1840)

United Nations (1968) Capital Punishment: Part I, Report 1960; Part II, Developments, 1961 to 1965. New York: United Nations.

*KATHY CALKINS CHARMAZ* is an assistant professor of sociology at California State College, Sonoma. Her interests include the sociology of death and the effect of illness upon the self.

# THE CORONER'S STRATEGIES FOR ANNOUNCING DEATH

### KATHY CALKINS CHARMAZ

INCREASINGLY IN AMERICAN SOCIETY, dying has become an institutionalized process through which deaths can be accounted for, counted, and routed through national standardized procedures performed by functionaries. It is assumed that dead persons must be identified, announced as deceased and removed from society. Accordingly, the county coroner's office is one organizational setting where dead individuals are processed through institutionalized procedures. Such processing is only completed by the coroner's office, however, when the person happens to have died under specified, usually somewhat atypical, circumstances. Consequently, informing the survivor of the death may pose some knotty interactional problems for the coroner who typically attempts to maintain a routine bureaucratic definition of his work.

The central problems dealt with in this paper focus on the methods coroner's deputies use to announce the death of a family member to unsuspecting survivors. The strategies they rely upon will be examined, particularly in relationship to those circumstances in which the "real" issue consists of handling the announcement in such a way that the family readily assumes

*AUTHOR'S NOTE:* Much of the data upon which this analysis is based was collected while I was working on Russell Sage Foundation grant #445210-58072, awarded to Anselm Strauss.

the costs of disposing of the body. Otherwise, the county must take on the costs. Attention is given to how the strategies serve to perpetuate the deputy's assumptions about human nature, grief, and personal responsibility. Finally, the construction of the strategies will be examined to show how the problematic features of interaction emerge and are controlled during the process of actual encounters.

## DATA AND METHODS

The major portion of the data is derived from open-ended interviews conducted with coroner's officials in three separate county departments within the same state. In each department, I obtained permission to talk with those individuals who had direct contact with the families of deceased persons who were "coroner's cases." Since the intent of the research was exploratory, questions were raised about the nature of their work, in addition to the kinds of concerns the deputies had about their encounters with families with whom they had contact. Although in this state the qualifications for serving as coroner or coroner's deputy vary widely, in the two more urbanized counties almost all the deputies held embalmer's licenses whereas in the rural county one out of four officials in the coroner's office possessed this license.[1] The rest were former sheriff's deputies.

The interview data are supplemented with materials from newspapers, county coroner's office reports, and urban league surveys, all of which provided background material on the kinds of cases that are examined. In each of the three counties studied, the coroner's office was situated in an urban area, although the counties varied in a number of their characteristics. County A covers a sprawling area with suburbs of all class levels as well as a major city of 500,000 containing a large population of urban poor. County B is (comparatively) of much greater density (750,000), although its geographical area is small; city and county boundaries are the same. County C is primarily a rural county, although the coroner's office is situated in a developing urban area of 62,000.

The data were analyzed in the context of their different social settings (J. Lofland, 1971). Comparisons were made between the structure of the county and how work is conducted. Further, the data were analyzed in relationship to the basic processes conducted in the everyday working world of the coroner's deputies. The method of analysis is the approach to grounded theory elaborated by Glaser and Strauss (1967). Characteristic of this approach, the data themselves provide the source of the categories which are developed. Initial categories and conjectures are subjected to testing while the researcher is still actively involved in field work. Consequently, the analysis is closely connected to the gathering of qualitative data and materials.

## THE INVESTIGATION PROCESS

In order to understand the relationship between announcing a death and the structure of the coroner's work, the investigation process will be described.

Investigation for the coroner's deputies revolves around four general areas: (1) ascertaining the cause of death, (2) establishing the identity of the deceased, (3) protecting the property of the deceased, and (4) discovering the identities of the relatives to whom the announcement of death must be made. All four aspects of the investigation process may be conducted simultaneously, since the deputy attempts to gather observations and information that provide clues in multiple facets of the case.

The process begins with all those cases that are reportable to the coroner. These range from routine deaths which simply occurred when the person was alone or without medical attendance, to accidental deaths, suicides, and homicides. Under some circumstances, the coroner may be directed to investigate cases that had been under medical supervision.[2] Increasingly greater numbers of cases are examined by the coroner's office.

The increases are directly related to sophisticated techniques of inquiry and medical examination.[3]

Reportable deaths differ from "coroner's cases." Coroner's cases are drawn from the pool of reportable deaths. However, conducting investigations to ascertain that a given case is surely *not* a coroner's case is a policy decision and is not obligatory. Deaths are defined as bona fide coroner's cases after the initial investigation by the deputy. The investigation consists of a review of medical records, questioning of any persons present for information, and an examination of the deceased's personal effects.

After gathering initial information, no further information may be deemed necessary. For example, a deputy described a case in which a woman had not been seen recently by a physician. He said, "All I had to do was read the medical history, there was no need to go further. She was full of cancer—there was no need to do an autopsy."

In urban coroner's offices, the deputies work in close cooperation with the medical examiner. The deputies compile information and search for clues which can be of assistance to the pathologist. For example, it may be necessary to know if the deceased was attempting to swallow food at the point when he collapsed or if he was taking any drugs at that time. Consequently, the deputies interview the relatives and/or bystanders to get the background information for leads for the pathologist to follow up.

Establishing the identity of the deceased is a critical aspect of the investigation process. Who is this person? When an individual dies in public without any identification cards, the investigation phase automatically requires much concerted effort on the part of the coroner's office, since it is ordinarily assumed that every effort will be made to identify the deceased and notify any relatives as soon as possible.

The intensity of the investigation to identify the victim and responsible relative is heightened when the death is defined as "news." In County A, in particular, deputies rush to beat the releases of news reports so that relatives will be spared undue shock. But in County B, the deputies use the news as a means of ferreting out more information. They defend their position on the basis that newsworthy stories consist only of nonroutine deaths. Hence, they may be able to discover the identity of the deceased through relatives' suspicions about his or her actual identity. Further, the deputies in this department may release information to the press in order to elicit some response. In short, the announcement of death may be strategically constructed in ways which maximize the efficient completion of the investigation by *reversing* the relationship in the announcement process such that notification is made by the relatives to the coroner's office.

Establishing the identity of the deceased is apt to be the most difficult in circumstances when young, out-of-town "hip" girls are murdered or commit suicide. Usual sources of clues tend to be minimal or nonexistent, since the deceased probably had few acquaintances and lacked identification cards. When clues are exhausted, identification is most likely to come from external sources such as an inquiry about a missing person or questions from an anxious parent who was struck by a news account of the death.

When the dead girl is acquainted with peers, however, the circumstances are more favorable for making a positive identification, since it is likely to be established simultaneously with the announcement of death. Again, in these circumstances, the relationship in the announcing process is reversed as coroners are notified by others, usually the parents. As one deputy revealed,

> Take a 17 or 18 year old girl who is stabbed in the H. district. She's probably never been finger-printed, has no record, no social security number, carries no identifying cards or letters. The group there *says* they only know her as "Mary"—they aren't going to tell the police anything. They *hate* the police. But actually they probably not only know her last name, but also where her parents are and their last names. So one of them will put in an anonymous call to the parents telling them what happened and where she is, then the parents will call us.

Frequently, routine investigations are conducted in the deceased's former premises in order to gain further clues and protect his or her property. This is, of course, most likely when the dead individual lived alone and is discovered in these premises.[4] Paradoxically, the same search which leads to the discovery of a relative and, not infrequently, a long-lost one at that, may later lead to conflict between the coroner's deputies and survivors. Conflict results over the valuables which relatives assume should be found in the deceased's possession, but which are not reported in the inventory compiled by the deputy after this search of the premises is finished.[5] Consequently, deputies are especially sensitive about the ways in which they disclose information to the relatives and handle the interaction when they are announcing the death.

Nonetheless, *locating* relatives is an important part of the investigation process, particularly in the most urbanized areas where finding them may prove arduous. The emphasis on locating a relative is heightened by the coroner's obligation to give relatives every opportunity to conduct religious services for the deceased, and moreover, to get them to assume the costs of burial. (In this state, should they be reluctant to do so, relatives may be sued by the coroner's office for three times the expense of burial in order to cover court costs.)

## THE ANNOUNCING PROCESS

Announcing the death, particularly to unsuspecting survivors, poses some interesting problems for the coroner's deputies— such as making the death credible, accountable, and acceptable to the relatives, as well as getting them to assume the cost burden. Those deputies who work in county departments where policies demand that announcements of death to survivors be made in person tend to acknowledge the problematic features of making such notifications. This contrasts with the county department where notification is made by phone. In either case, the deputies develop strategies, which will be discussed below, for handling problematic features of announcing the death to relatives. The different techniques in handling the situation reflect different ideologies and organizational practices.

## Structural Conditions and the Announcing Process

Although coroner's deputies in each of the three counties performed similar duties, the character of the announcing process varied according to the structural conditions of their work. A key variable appears to be the availability of funds or alternatives for assuming the costs of disposing of the body. Thus, the tenacity with which coroner's deputies will conduct an investigation leading to the discovery of a heretofore unknown relative appears to correspond to the financial resources of the county for providing inexpensive burials. Correspondingly, the beliefs espoused by coroner's deputies as to what their role *should be* in the announcing process are based in part on assumptions about financial responsibility. For example, county burial in one county was approximately $200 more than in another; and in the former county, coroner's deputies espouse beliefs that maximize the financial responsibility of the deceased's relatives. In the counties where cheap public burials were more available, relatives were much less pressured to assume the costs. As the deputy supervisor in County B (which has access to cheap burials) commented:

> If it is some bum who died and you have to call back in Ohio to people who haven't seen him for years—I tell them: "If you don't have money, don't do it." Why should they get stuck with an expensive funeral . . . even an inexpensive one is too much for some families.

So, too, the strategies employed in announcing the death to relatives differ according to whether or not getting them to pay for burial costs is defined as necessary. When it is defined as necessary and therefore, an important part of the deputy's work, special techniques are likely to be invoked. When successful, making the announcement in person has the practical consequence of increasing the probability that an uneventful and speedy disposition of the body will be made at the expense of the family.

## Self-Protection Strategies

Self-protection strategies are employed to maintain the *routine* character of the work and to keep the deputy from feeling involved in the on-going scene. Clearly, the "distance" deputies place between themselves and death is potentially diminished while they are involved in making the announcement of death. As they announce the death to the closest relative, possibilities arise for questions and concerns to be raised which might force the deputies to reflect upon death. Although deputies are more directly confronted with issues concerning death than most persons in everyday worlds, they disavow holding any unusual views or beliefs about the topic. Indeed, what is striking is the degree to which their views reflect typical cultural taboos. For the most part, deputies show an avoidance of death, discomfiture over the expression of grief by survivors, and an absence of personal philosophy about death in general or subjective views regarding their own deaths in particular.

Nonetheless, deputies have built up a set of fairly consistent beliefs which serve to perpetuate strategies which protect them from entertaining new ideas about death. An integral part of these beliefs is the view that death is an *external* event which is almost completely separate from their everyday worlds. Death then becomes subjectively interpreted by the deputies as being the incidental source of their work—a by-product of the work rather than the focus of it. The deputies appear to feel compelled to protect themselves from confronting other meanings about the relationship between their work and death. Hence, a main source of self-protection is based on the deputies' emphasis on the routine aspects of the work as the "real" activity. Constructing this definition of reality takes continued effort and is particularly problematic when the deputy is either with the deceased or the bereaved relatives.

The extent to which death is externalized and separated from the subjective consciousness of the deputy is exemplified by one deputy's statement: "That's not a body lying there. It's an *investigation*. You have to look at it as an investigation, not as a person lying there." By constructing the definition of the deceased as an "investigation," the deputy is able to maintain his definition of the situation and, moreover, to perpetuate his view of death as external and separate from himself.

Occupational ideologies held by the deputies support this view of death, since it is generally believed that becoming involved in the situation prevents one from functioning properly in his duties. Since this view of death is shared and reaffirmed, it serves as a way of protecting the deputy from experiencing the deaths he encounters in ways other than those which are officially prescribed. Not surprisingly, in the smallest county—where the deputy's chances of personal acquaintance with the deceased is much greater than in the larger counties, if the identity of the deceased is established and he is recognized as an acquaintance—self-protection is enhanced by sending out the other officer on duty. Similarly, in an office with several men on duty, a deputy confessed to attempting to avoid notifying young wives of the deaths of their husbands, since these were cases he had difficulty treating routinely. In circumstances such as these, deputies believe, the parameters of the "proper" amount of involvement might be exceeded and their potential "effectiveness" in the situation lost.

An aspect of self-protection consists of the effort to remain the polite, sincere, authoritative, but basically disinterested official. This stance becomes particularly apparent when the deputy's taken-for-granted notions of how the relative should respond are disrupted or negated. When the relative is lacking the usual proprieties of such occasions or fails to show the "proper" expression of grief, the deputy may feel constrained to normalize the situation for *himself* instead of for the relative. An example was given by a deputy whose taken-for-granted notions about grief were upset when he informed a young wife of her husband's death several hours before in a traffic accident. She said, "It couldn't have happened to a nicer guy, and I'm not sorry." Another example was provided by the same deputy who recalled a parent who seemed almost detached and said only, "That poor little son-of-a-bitch."

When the relative appears to take the "bad news" with so little seeming affect, the deputy then has to make sense of the situation in order to integrate the discrepant information into his own view of reality. His relationship to the relative is apt to shift as he tries to discover information that helps make the response he has witnessed sensible and accountable. Thus, he himself may be in the position of experiencing initial disbelief and lack of comprehension when the encounter precludes the successful use of his usual self-protection strategies. Moreover, having his taken-for-granted assumptions upset may cause the deputy to confront questions about the meaning of death that undermine his usual routinization of work.

## Assumptions Underlying the Strategies

Strategies for making different types of announcements rest on central assumptions about human nature and the meaning of grief. These assumptions are logically connected to the deputies' conceptions of what constitute *acceptable conventions* for dealing "appropriately" with the relatives when announcing the death to them.

Two divergent views of human nature appear in the data. One emphasized human weakness in the face of crisis; the other, rationality and human strength. Deputies in Counties A and C took for granted a concept of human nature in which the individual is fragile and weak in the face of crisis. They carried an image of persons as unstable and easily overwhelmed when confronted with personal loss of a loved one. Consequently, they felt that breaking such ominous and significant news to the family required special skills. They assumed that the survivors had need of artfully provided social support, and they often observed that policemen tended to be too blunt and tough to handle such delicate situations appropriately and tactfully. They pointed to the bewilderment of a parent when a policeman comes to the door and greets him with "Your son is dead," or simply hands the parent a card with the county coroner's phone number on it and makes no announcement at all. One deputy implied that the uniform alone was sufficient reason not to send a law enforcement officer. He felt that the "shock of seeing a *uniform* come to the door, especially in the middle of the night, would be too much for the family."

Furthermore, these deputies assumed that the time and tact they took with the family would be viewed by anyone as the preferable way to break the news. They believed that they were, in a sense, participating in the experience of the family during the moment of shock and horror when the announcement is made. Through their participation, the deputies saw themselves as lending the family member, however briefly, some emotional support and protection by, for example, making sure, before leaving, that the relative was with someone and had food available.

This type of service is stressed by deputies who felt that the shock of a sudden death alone could be disastrous for the survivor. One deputy remarked,

> When you go to that house, you don't know who or what you are dealing with. You've already got one death, you don't need another. Maybe the wife—or husband—has a heart condition or is under a doctor's care or needs tranquilizers. Your job is to make sure the relative's alright.

Thus, according to this perspective, the intrusion of privacy resulting from the presence of the deputy as he makes his critical announcement is mitigated by the help he gives. Moreover, implicit in the deputy's perspective, is the symbolic message he gives that there is still some order and authority in what he thinks the survivors might view as a suddenly chaotic world.

This view of human nature contrasts quite radically with that espoused by the Chief Coroner in County B and echoed by his deputies. He maintains that people are more rational and sensible than they are credited as being:

> Many think we are cruel and inhuman [he means the press and on-lookers by "many"], but they have a strange idea of human nature. People are far more reasonable than given credit for.

This view stresses the beliefs that (1) people can adapt to crisis situations without mishap, (2) they can indeed function in their various capacities during a crisis, and (3) they desire personal *privacy* when experiencing a crisis.

Several significant implications emerge from this conception of human nature. The first concerns the appropriate way in which death announcements should be made. With their stress on the rationality of human beings, these deputies posit the belief that the survivor will want to know as soon as possible and, therefore, it is obligatory for the deputy to phone them immediately. If the deputy cannot reach them himself, it makes little difference if the office clerks do so. For that matter, the services of others—typically an employer, clergyman, or police-man—are elicited to break the news when it is more convenient for them to do so. Considerations are made for the survivor's privacy when others are drafted, as well as the heavy time demands on the deputy. For example, if a wife is at work when her husband collapses on the freeway, the deputy is likely to arrange for her employer to inform her of the news in some private place. As a sidelight, even if the deputy had the time to visit the survivor at home, he might be somewhat hesitant to do so, since he is in his uniform and driving an identifiable vehicle and his very presence symbolizes crisis and draws the attention of an audience of on-lookers at a time when he believes the individual he visits wants privacy and anonymity.

Central assumptions about the meaning of grief also differed. Deputies in Counties A and C, where announcements were made in person, defined grief as a *genuine reaction* which could be expected, though they often thought it paralyzing to the bereaved. They assumed that family ties were usually meaningful, and death could represent a grave emotional loss to the survivor. Moreover, these deputies appeared to take the fright some people expressed over being forced to rechannel their own lives without their spouses as a natural part of grieving. And by tacitly acknowledging it, they shared in the grieving. Consider the statement of the deputy supervisor:

> You go tell the wife. Maybe she's pregnant and got two already and you know they live from one check to another and you just see it go across her face, "What am I going to do now?" It really makes you feel bad. Often they have no insurance. That sort of hangs on my mind for a while; what will this young wife do?

In contrast, officials in County B tended to view grief as both *problematic and troublesome.* The head coroner said, "We have a saying around here that 'Grief lasts as long as the flowers take to wilt.' The other is display." These coroners stressed the showmanship that they believed was exhibited around death. Several of them remarked that people took it well, as long as they had no audience; as soon as somebody entered the scene, weeping and wailing would rapidly ensue. The Head Coroner illustrated his point with the following anecdote:

> Some years ago, the deputies picked up a Mexican whose brother was notified and told to be there at the time of the search. They found the brother weeping and wailing and hitting his head against the wall. After waiting for him to subside for a while, they began to search anyway, even though he was still hitting his head against the wall—the relative is always supposed to be present and attentive to what is going on during the search. When they pulled out the man's wallet, the brother jumped up, said, "I'll take that," [grabbed it] then went back to hitting his head against the wall after he grabbed the wallet.

Note that this view of grief assumes that actual or real grief lasts only for a short time for *anyone,* despite cultural experience or subjective interpretations. This perspective presupposes that people can create alternatives, if they do not already have them, for sudden changes in their lives.

In this viewpoint, grief is related to selfishness and fear. They define grieving family members, especially wives, as being much more likely to be concerned with their own fates—the consequences the death will have for them—than sorrow over the loss of a significant other. The way in which these coroners defined grief negates the notion of submerging one's identity into the identity of a spouse. A particular view of women was tacitly espoused. That is, women should not be so dependent upon their husbands in the first place and should adapt to widowhood without causing problems for themselves, society, and the coroner's office. In the extreme articulation of their perspective, the joining of psychological selves or the immersion of self of the wife into her husband's life was not considered. To illustrate, the Head Coroner voiced the opinion, "Chances are, the old lady didn't give a hoot for him anyway and is glad he is gone."

Quite clearly, the central assumptions about human nature and grief have practical consequences for the everyday world of work in a coroner's office. Given all the assumptions made by deputies in Counties A and C, it logically follows that announcing the death in person would fit their conceptions of acceptable conventions for handling the task. Not to do so would not only constitute a breach of ethics, but to them would imply *trivializing* what they define as a significant task.

In contrast, officials in County B think that such conventions for handling death practices are unnecessary and outmoded. Specifically, they felt that personal announcements are an anachronism stemming from military tradition which somehow became imbedded in our common-sense notions. In turn, they feel that this mode of notification is rooted in "vicious taboos" about death that encouraged people to commit themselves to courses of action they do not actually endorse and magnify the amount of material and emotional "false display." Consequently, they believe that their technique of formalistic telephone notification is a more acceptable convention in our urbanized society.

## The Strategies for Announcing

Strategies for making the announcement help the deputy remain in control of the situation and handle the special problems which emerge in the course of interaction. Not the least of these problems is the necessity of the deputy to construct the *contextual properties* of the announcing scene, in addition to constructing the announcement itself. In other words, he must create the kind of ambience and interactional circumstance wherein the announcement logically fits so that it is effective and believable; he has no ready-made scene to serve as an official backdrop for his proclamation.[6]

Since he essentially has no organizational props or dramaturgical aids to create the proper atmosphere of the scene at his disposal, the deputy strategically manages the encounter so that the scene is built up through his use of impression management and strategic disclosure of cues (Goffman, 1959 and 1972). Compared to the physician who makes the announcement of "bad news" to the relative, the deputy has a weighty problem. Given his much lesser amount of authority and prestige, the deputy also lacks the advantages typically possessed by the physician of a prior relationship with the relative, a fitting organizational setting for giving the news, and a series of prior interactional cues which serve to prepare the relative (Sudnow, 1967).

Since the deputy has neither the structural supports provided by the hospital situation, nor the physician's status, he has to devise tactics to get his work done without incident. Typically, his objectives are to announce quickly, to turn the responsibility of the body and its subsequent burial expense over to the family, and to determine that the person who received the news is holding up well or is with someone. But all these tasks may be embellishments to his main task of disposition of the body and getting the family to assume the expenses when this is his major or real objective.[7]

The deputy's first strategic maneuver is to make certain that he has contacted the correct person. Since high transience rates exist in parts of urban centers, the deputy may, at times, feel quite compelled to ascertain that he has reached the right person. Similarly, when the announcement is made by telephone, the deputy must first ask if he actually has the party to whom he requested to speak.

Once he is assured that the correct person has been located, he must then ensure that the relative accepts *his* identity as real. Thus, a potential problem for the deputy, one that occasionally arises, is the refusal of the relative to recognize him as a bona fide member of the coroner's office and the bearer of bad news. Consequently, through the use of gestures, tone of voice, and body positioning, the deputy attempts to create a first impression of himself that will set the tone of the following encounter (cf. Schwartz, 1974).

A useful strategy that some deputies employ, particularly when they have previously confronted the issue of nonrecognition, is to take a neighbor with them. The deputy will first attempt to locate the neighbor who is most known to the survivor. Then he will explain to the neighbor that the situation will be somewhat eased if a person who is known and trusted is present.

This stated reason for utilizing a neighbor is, primarily, a justification for more practical motives. First, the neighbor's accompaniment helps to establish the deputy's identity by demonstrating that the neighbor has already accepted it as real. Further, in anticipation of the possibility that the relative may not permit strangers to enter his or her home, the deputy protects himself from refusal; thus, entry into the home is not difficult. In addition, the neighbor serves as a buttress for the staging of the scene to follow. The concern and gravity written on the neighbor's face quickly cues the survivor that this is, in fact, a very serious occasion. Then, as the deputy introduces himself and his job affiliation, "They know what is coming."

From the perspective of the deputy, however, the most advantageous aspect of this strategy is that by virtue of the neighbor's presence, the deputy is not detained; he can get out almost immediately.

Cues are similarly built up when the deputy is unaccompanied or notifies by phone. One deputy said that he tried to talk to the relative for a few minutes before making the announcement. He said, "I ask if they have received any phone calls about the member of the family before telling them." The timing of cues is also controlled by officials who phone, identify themselves, but not their office, since they think that they should give the relative a few cues of lesser weight before getting to the point of the call. They prefer to stall slightly by giving some general statements concerning the fact that they are informing the relative of very serious news. In this way, they strategically set the circumstances wherein the relative will attend to the deputy's interpretation of the news. A deputy supervisor noted that he usually tells them, "I have some terrible news for you," and then repeats his statement, before going on to construct the actual announcement.

In both situations, as he prepares to move into the announcement, the deputy creates the context by rapidly giving one meaningful cue after another which brings the relative into interaction. Compared to the medical scene, the cues come much more rapidly and sharply. Thus, the cues cannot be easily dismissed, although the survivor has little time to think about them.[8]

The skillful deputy can be expected to handle the situation in such a way that cues will neither be missed nor misinterpreted. The relative is not permitted enough time to dis-attend to them and, should they attempt to do so, the deputy will alter his presentation accordingly. For example, a deputy stated, "Sometimes I'm stern, sometimes I'm sympathetic, sometimes I even shout a little bit louder than they can."

Those deputies who telephone find they get a better response when they successively lead the relatives into questioning *them.*

By doing so, the official sets the conditions wherein he can impart progressively unpromising news. For example:

> I tell them that he collapsed today while at work. They asked if he is alright now. I say slowly, "Well, no, but they took him to the hospital." They ask if he is there now. I say, "They did all they could do—the doctors tried very hard." They say, "He is dead at the hospital?" Then I tell them he's at the coroner's office.

Most deputies expressly avoid the word "dead" when first imparting the news, since they feel it is too harsh. Substitutes are used such as "fatally injured" and "passed away," if they must make direct reference to it at all. A preferred technique is to control the interaction so that the relative refers to the person as "dead." Those making telephone announcements attempt to manipulate the conversation so that the relative says the word, "dead." Several deputies remarked that having the survivors themselves say it made the announcement more meaningful to them, and the death more "real." Describing a close family member as "dead" cuts through the relative's prior shock or disbelief. And the survivor's reference to his or her relative as "dead" becomes symbolic and sets the stage for treating the deceased as such. The deputy then reaffirms the survivor's statements and elaborates on the theme. Consequently, when the deputy's strategies work, the transition from perceiving one's relative as alive to dead can be made rapidly. The symbolic shift is likely to occur so quickly during the encounter that the relative may remain unaware of how the interaction was managed. Indeed, in an encounter the deputy deems successful, the relative is likely to express appreciation for his "sensitivity."

Deputies state that the relatives always ask about the circumstances of dying. The coroner gives them what information he has and can release, then turns the situation around by asking about funeral and burial arrangements. To illustrate: "They always ask what happened. Then we reverse it and ask what type of arrangements *they* are going to make."

Or, in the case of the telephone notification, the relative typically inquires, "What can I do (to help)?" The deputy simply states, "All you need do now is call your family funeral director; and he'll direct you." In both situations, this approach gets the relative down to business and usually results in his or her agreement to "help," while still in the midst of the initial encounter with the deputy. Likely, the relative has unwittingly volunteered to underwrite the expenditures before he has any conception of the implications or the expense of this. Simultaneously, the deputy has played the role of the official who cuts through the survivor's grief and shock by pointing to the work that has to be done. As the relative becomes aware of what he has committed himself to, he or she may ask the deputy about the deceased's resources (if not already known). Here again the deputy has the opportunity to define what is happening and that the responsibility, until proven otherwise, lies with the family.

## CONCLUSION

The ways in which the coroner's deputies conduct their work sheds light on aspects of urban life that are not within the purview of the ordinary citizen. How work is conducted appears to reflect the character of the urban milieu in which a given coroner's department operates. For example, County B is known as being a cosmopolitan area in which anonymity and privacy are more characteristic than in either Counties A or C, which have the feeling of being small towns grown large. In these counties, traditions reminiscent of smaller towns where personal acquaintances and stability of residence still obtain. Perhaps then, taken-for-granted customs reflecting these traditions are practiced by the coroners.

More importantly, the relationship the deputy has with a survivor is, initially at least, that of a stranger (cf. L. Lofland, 1973). But this relationship has some special properties, since the setting where the encounter ensues is located in the private world of the survivor. In addition, the kind of interaction taking place is characterized by its intensity, rapidity of sequence, and strategic control manipulated by the deputy. Since the deputy controls information that is vital to the survivors but of a routine nature to the deputy, the properties of their interaction provide a fertile field of study for the sociologist.

## NOTES

1. Structural conditions, such as the size of the community served by department and what other agency or community liaisons the coroner's department has, have much to do with how the coroner's office is organized. For example, in one area the coroner may be a one-man department which is simply an off-shoot of the sheriff's department. Here the coroner may do all the initial inquiry and record-keeping himself, then obtain consultations with pathologists when he finds it necessary. In many areas, the half-time coroner also serves as the town mortician. In contrast, in highly urbanized areas, the coroner's office develops into a public service remaining more independent of other city offices, although, at times, work is completed with the close cooperation of other city agencies and organizations.

2. Specifically, the state code directs the coroner to investigate deaths that occur under medical supervision when (1) the physician is unable or unwilling to establish the cause of death, (2) death occurs in surgery, (3) death occurs before the patient has recovered from an anesthetic, and (4) death follows a coma.

3. For some intriguing comments about the implications of the varied amounts of skill that are evidenced in different coroner's departments, see Douglas (1971: 96-98).

4. Since part of the work of the coroner consists of "protecting" the property of the deceased, they may close up the house of an unmarried couple, since by law all the effects go to the next of kin, even if that person is a spouse from whom the deceased has long been separated.

5. For a newspaper account affirming the notion of questionable practices by deputies, see the *San Francisco Chronicle* (1975)—the sentencing of a coroner's deputy charged with stealing a $100 money order from a dead woman.

6. For an analysis of how a backdrop can essentially pre-announce the event to follow, see Fred Davis' (1972) account of the candlelight engagement ceremony of student nurses.

7. In some areas, simply getting the family to assume the expenses is not enough for the coroner, since—if he has vested interests in a local mortuary—he may through subtle or obvious means direct them toward these services. Such practices are, of course, ethically questionable. Just such an incident occurred in Contra Costa County, where the mortician's helpers were the coroner's ambulance drivers. Consequently, the coroner and his deputies and associated funeral homes were sued

for $900,000 by other local funeral directors. See the *San Francisco Chronicle* (1968).

8. Cues also come rapidly and sharply when people are announcing good news, although it may be the case that the news was already anticipated in the event of a forthcoming marriage or a birth. However, it is doubtful that the announcer takes the pains to strategize in the same ways as above, or to create a context and control the interaction in such explicit ways.

# REFERENCES

DAVIS, F. (1972) "Rituals of annunciation: on the good fortune of getting married, or symbolism vs. functionalism," pp. 39-55 in F. Davis, Illness, Interaction and the Self. Belmont, Calif.: Wadsworth.

DOUGLAS, J. D. (1971) American Social Order. New York: Free Press.

GLASER, B. G. and A. L. STRAUSS (1967) The Discovery of Grounded Theory. Chicago: Aldine.

GOFFMAN, E. (1972) Strategic Interaction. New York: Ballantine.

——— (1959) The Presentation of Self in Everyday Life. Garden City, N.Y.: Doubleday-Anchor.

LOFLAND, J. (1971) Analyzing Social Settings. Belmont, Calif.: Wadsworth.

LOFLAND, L. H. (1973) A World of Strangers. New York: Basic Books.

San Francisco Chronicle (1975) "Coroner's aide is sentenced." February 26: 16.

——— (1968) "$900,000 morticians trade suit." July 20: 6.

SCHWARTZ, H. (1974) "First impressions." Berkeley: University of California. (unpublished manuscript)

SUDNOW, D. (1967) Passing On: The Social Organization of Dying. Englewood Cliffs, N.J.: Prentice-Hall.

*JABER F. GUBRIUM* is Associate Professor of Sociology at Marquette University in Milwaukee. He does research and has published a number of articles in the areas of aging, patient care, and the sociology of the life cycle. His book, *Living and Dying at Murray Manor,* was published in 1975 by St. Martin's Press, New York. Currently, he is working on a book that takes a social phenomenological approach to the life cycle.

# DEATH WORLDS IN A NURSING HOME

## JABER F. GUBRIUM

ALL FORMALLY ORGANIZED social settings have main events. These are commonly recognized acts or act sequences that are considered both officially and unofficially characteristic by setting members. For example, the taking of communion within some churches, collective bargaining in the automobile industry, and the solitary confinement of an inmate in prison are all main events. Main events stand in contrast to minor ones in that the latter—making and taking bets on horses on an assembly line or shooting craps in the back wards of a mental hospital, for example—are recognized as characteristic of the setting only by some of the members.

Although all members of a social setting recognize a main event as characteristic of it, this does not imply that they all perceive and consider it in the same way. All may be able to talk about it, but not all talk is tacitly grounded in the same definition. Insofar as the setting has a differentiated structure, multiple definitions of main events are likely to exist. Defini-

*AUTHOR'S NOTE:* Field work for this study was supported by a Summer Faculty Fellowship, Marquette University, Milwaukee, Wisconsin.

tions of main events are bound to the perspectives of actors occupying various positions in it. Subworlds of meaning coexist within a socially differentiated universe (cf. Berger and Luckmann, 1966: 79-82).

Given that actors are not completely constrained by the setting to act in particular ways, variations in their definitions of main events are related to what they do about them. The behavioral contingencies of their worlds are closely linked with their definitional realities (cf. Thomas, 1966: 117-191). Behavioral outcomes of various definitions are all "normal" modes of action to the extent that definitions constitute taken-for-granted conceptions of events.

In this paper, dying and death are examined as main events in a nursing home setting. Two problems are considered: (1) definitions of dying and death in the nursing home as they vary with structured differences between actors (death worlds), and (2) the manner in which these variations in definition are linked to what actors do about dying and death in relation to themselves and each other within the organizational setting (death work).

Two aspects of the nursing home as a socially differentiated organization affect how actors deal with their definitions of main events in relation to those of others. First, the mere fact that there is social differentiation between actors, and that such differences make for a variety of perspectives on dying and death, means that when persons carrying different views of these events interact, they may not be acting on the basis of common tacit understandings. Second, not only do structured differences influence the dying and death work of actors, but so does structured order. Authority affects who is likely to accommodate whom in dealing with main events. Although lower staff members may define dying and death differently from members holding top staff positions, it is the lower staff that accommodates its superiors. This, however, occurs only when the lower staff is directly accountable to superiors, namely, when the latter preside over main events. The relevant acts of main events are to some extent defined by actors' awareness of who is participating in them in any particular situation.

In dealing with their own and others' definitions of main events, actors make use of physical resources available in their social setting. Depending on their situated presence or nonavailability, such physical contingencies of a social setting as halls, empty rooms, and doors may support or discredit actors' attempts to deal with death worlds. The physical arrangements of a social setting affect the credibility of work that actors do to maintain the order of various worlds of dying and death.

The social order of dying and death does not lie completely in the officially organized system of social relations around these events. When actors feel no need to support a certain patterning of events, they alter their acts. In relevant situations, actors work to sustain certain patterns of social order (Glaser and Strauss, 1965: 14-15; Goffman, 1971: 62-187; Douglas, 1973: 109). The social orders of dying and death are constructed and abandoned, sometimes rather fortuitously (Blumer, 1969), as different actors and their definitions accomplish various social and physical situations in an organized setting.

## ORGANIZATIONAL SETTING

Murray Manor is a 360-bed, nonprofit nursing home located in a middle-sized midwestern city. It has six floors, the lowest two of which have been reserved for persons in need of only residential care, while the upper four are scheduled to house those in need of various levels of skilled nursing care. These persons are referred to, respectively, as residents and patients. Together they constitute the clientele of the home.

At the time data were gathered,[1] Murray Manor's census fluctuated around 130. One-third of these were residents and the others patients. Residents occupied the first floor and patients were housed on floors three and four. The mean age of residents and patients was about 80 years. The organization referred to itself officially as a "geriatric care facility."

*Patients and residents:* The clientele of Murray Manor, taken together, constitute one of the role complexes which generates particular definitions of dying and death. When dying or death occurs in the nursing home, it is clientele who physically *experience* either or both. Every day, patients and residents live with the situated contingency that dying and death are imminent events for them.

Not only do patients and residents experience dying or death, but each also is a frequent *witness* to the experiences of others. If he is not seriously experiencing either, he still sees what he might easily become by observing persons around him who are vividly dying or who are dead. Thus, when he anticipates his own ending, he does so in terms of those life endings he has seen.

The position of client differs from other positions in relation to dying and death in that all its incumbents minimally experience and daily witness these as main events. Persons in other positions in the nursing home may witness these events, but they do not themselves experience them. The combination of experiencing and witnessing generates a death world that differs from that of persons whose positions do not combine both.

Residents and patients are not exactly alike as far as the continuity of experiencing and witnessing dying. Persons become or are admitted as patients at Murray Manor when staff defines them as showing "obvious" signs of potentially dying. Both staff and clientele believe all clients to be minimally terminal in that they are aged, reside in the nursing home, and are not fully expected to return to society "out there." Patients, however, more commonly show certain visible ("pointable") signs of dying than residents; for example, they may be bedridden, bound to wheelchairs, or virtually unintelligible. Residents experience only minimal and periodically vivid episodes of dying. Some have occasional epileptic seizures. Others have mild heart attacks or chest pains. Most take medications for nondisabling, but chronic illnesses. Yet, although patients and residents experience dying in varying degrees, they all define their futures in terms of death. In that respect, they are all dying.

Patients tend to witness dying continuously. Residents, on the other hand, witness dying in only four kinds of situations. When one of them experiences an occasional crisis, such as a seizure or heart attack, this is considered by other residents to be an event in which "he [or she] could have died." Second, if the crisis is disabling to the degree that the person affected needs skilled nursing care, he is transferred to the third or fourth floor and becomes a patient. Third, the physical arrangements of several services at Murray Manor make it necessary for those residents desiring to use them to risk observing dying patients. For example, the beauty and barber shop is located on the third floor, which houses patients. Fourth, for about ten months, two residents had wives on the third floor. Their daily reports to other residents on the health status of their wives contributed to vicarious witnessing of dying among those who listened. Another kind of vicarious witnessing occurs when residents inform others on the first floor of the status of patients who are their personal friends and whom they occasionally visit on the third and fourth floors.

There are also differences between patients and residents in the extent to which each experiences or witnesses death. Both patients and residents believe that patients are more likely to die than residents. References are often made to "the fact that up there [here], you're likely to go any time." Death is considered a more common event on the third and fourth floors than it is on the first. However, because of their ambulatory accessibility and the physical arrangements of the nursing home, residents are more likely to witness death than patients, especially more than bedridden ones. The social contacts that depend on ambulatory accessibility mean that when one resident hears about a death in the home, all of them are likely to know of it in short order.

*Floor staff:* A second complex of roles within the nursing home setting is the floor staff. It consists of nurses and nurses' aides who spend all of their time working with patients on the floors. Nurses' aides are the members of the floor staff who have the most direct and continuous contact with patients. They are responsible for bed-and-body work—namely, feeding, voiding, changing beds, and washing bodies. On the resident floor, the staff is much less extensive. Here, there normally is one person in charge, who may be a nurse but, more often, is officially defined and appears dressed as a hostess.

Members of the floor staff do not personally experience dying and death. They are, however, more frequent witnesses of both than patients and residents. Since they work with patients and residents, they witness the variety of dyings and deaths that occur among all of them. Not only is the floor staff witness to more dying and death, but it witnesses it more intimately than either patients or residents. For example, floor staff must handle and peruse such evidence of dying as extreme emaciation and extensive physical decay. Patients and residents may observe these, but they never handle or treat them. Witnessing dying and death is an integral part of the floor staff's routine work with patients and residents. As one aide stated, "You get used to even the worst ones when you work around them a while." It is a routine part of work to care for extreme cases of both ambulatory and terminal patients.

*Top staff:* A third complex of roles that generates a particular world of death is the administrative or top staff. Within the top staff are such positions as administrator, social worker, medical director, chaplain, director and assistant director of nursing, in-service director, occupational therapist, and activity director. Persons occupying these positions formulate various kinds of formal and informal policy, one category of which pertains to dying and death Those most directly responsible for establishing dying and death policy are the administrator and the director of nursing.

Like the floor staff, top staff does not personally experience dying and death. However, in contrast to the floor staff, neither does it witness dying and death to any great extent, nor does it extensively witness patient and resident responses to either. Most of top staff's time is taken up with administrative matters which not only concern internal routines in the nursing home but relations with the public. This keeps its members off the patient floors. When top staff personnel do appear on the floors, their business usually does not directly involve the care of patients and residents. Rather, they appear because they have administrative duties there.

The witnessing of death by top staff is not primarily a matter of considering or working directly with the dead and other clientele, but rather presiding over floor staff's work with them. A top staff nurse verifies a floor nurse's death diagnosis, calls the physician, and obtains a death pronouncement. The administrator manages the death scene both in terms of space and timing. He sees to it that all floor personnel are properly involved and patients distant. He may supervise the entire sequencing of events from death to removal of the body. The chaplain may perform a variety of religious rituals.

## DEATH WORLDS

Death worlds are behavioral definitions. They are ways of thinking about the main events of dying and death, which constitute the practical reality of the events for those persons holding them. To the extent that the everyday lives of persons in any organized setting are socially differentiated, variations in conceptions of the world are generated.

### Patients and Residents

For patients and residents, talk about dying is never completely separate from talk of death. They do not have a set of opinions and feelings about one that is separate from the other. Both in their own conversations and in interviews at Murray Manor, it was rarely possible to discuss either alone.

Dying and death talk among patients and residents in many informal situations at Murray Manor show evidence of how these events are linked in their minds. Patients or residents gathered in a parlor exchange opinions about dying and death whenever one of them mentions that he "just happened to look in on" or "heard about" a dying person. Typically, the exchange of opinions involves at least two kinds of statements. First, someone or all say that the suffering is terribly depressing. Sometimes, one adds that either the dying person is "taking it very hard" or "taking it very well." Second, talk of death always closes the conversation. This usually takes one of two forms, depending on whether discussion has turned to their own futures or is still oriented to the dying person. When it becomes centered on their own futures, comments are made about the personal desirability of death, should one begin "really" suffering (dying). When it is still oriented to the dying person, one is likely to hear, "Death would be a blessing for him," or "I hope she passes for her sake, the poor thing."

For patients and residents, then, the world of death includes both dying and death. Death is conceived as the endpoint of dying. This is one dimension of their death world. A second dimension is their evaluation of the dying process. Although the death world of patients and residents includes both, death is considered a more desirable state than dying. This is true both for visibly dying patients and for other patients and residents. For example:

> Who likes life, anyhow. Well, it's just that I wanna pass away. That's the one. I wanna pass away. That's it. Well, what should I do? The rest of the afternoon I don't know what I'm gonna do. God help me. I wanna go. I'd like to pass away. It would be quiet and nice.

> I'm bad and they're worse yet. So, why a person has to live that kind of life? If you're old, you should die and be done with it. They're no good to nobody. They're just like a vegetable. I hope some day I go to sleep and I don't get up. I only ask God to give me peace as soon as possible. Take me out of this world.

There is a third dimension to patients' and residents' death world—namely, both patients and residents talk rather perfunctorily about death in general. Dying patients matter-of-factly describe its characteristics in terms opposite to what they consider the most prominent features of dying. If dying for them means pain, death becomes blissful relief. If living means being a burden to others, death means quiet solitude. Residents and patients tend to describe the character of death more uniformly than do visibly dying patients. Since dying, for them, indicates chronic dependence, death is simply the "end of useless living."

One exception to this occurs when patients and residents talk about a close or intimate friend who died.[2] For example, when a patient's or resident's close friend dies, he usually refers to the death mournfully. Such persons typically mention that they miss the deceased and that they are somewhat in despair at the loss. A resident recalls her friend this way:

> There's one that died from this floor. She came the same day I did. She was Miss Custer. She'd never been married. She was a school teacher. She was a very nice person, and real friendly. I miss her. I'm really sorry that she's gone. She was as lonesome as I was. I was alone. So we used to visit each other. Yes, I liked her very much. I felt awful bad when she died.

And a male patient stated:

> Oh, not unless he's a personal friend. Otherwise, I don't give a damn. Of course, I feel it because I know it's a life, but it doesn't affect you that much. Now George [roommate who's his friend] . . . if there's anything wrong with George, I would feel sorry for him. I like George, and I think he's a hell of a nice fella.

Talk of dying, in contrast, is much less perfunctory than talk of death, for both patients and residents. Patients who are dying are likely to weep in commenting about it. Their descriptions are expressive, vivid, and notably punctuated by urgent comparisons with persons who are healthier. Some are abrupt and point to themselves, as one woman did and said, "Look! This is dying!" Residents become somewhat agitated in talking about dying. Most try to rush over it.

## Floor Staff

When floor staff works with patients and residents, it takes account of what it believes is their relative alertness. What members of the floor staff talk about and what they do in the presence of persons in their charge depends on how alert they define such persons to be. When patients present in some situation are considered alert, floor staff will avoid making mention of anyone who has died. Being alert, to floor staff, means that one has personal death sensibilities. Alert patients and residents, floor staff believes, are in many ways just like themselves as persons. Both are considered to share a felt morbidity and anxiousness about their own deaths. When deaths are discussed in the nursing home, however, it is always assumed to be a patient or resident death. Thus, floor staff refrains from openly mentioning death in the company of alert patients or residents.

Among patients not considered to be alert (or, as staff would say, either "senile," "confused," or "disoriented"), floor staff talks openly about death. Such talk is clearly audible to these patients. Moreover, it is often quite descriptive and glib. It is not uncommon to hear aides shout to each other across a patient's room, asking if some recently dead person's body has been prepared yet. Typically, the responding aide will answer yes or no, or list what else is to be done, if the body has been only partially prepared. This may include mention of any of the following: changing bedding due to fecal or urine soiling; washing the body; removing such personal belongings as glasses, rings, or watches; and retaining or removing dentures from the deceased's mouth.

Open talk about dying, however, is not contingent on the believed alertness of patients. Regardless of what kind of patient or resident is present, floor staff will converse about the bed-and-body work it has completed and what yet remains to be done. Aides will tell or ask each other to do or help with such work as changing bedding, lifting heavy patients, turning them for decubiti, and taking those who are incapacitated to toilet. Such talk is rarely strained. It is considered to be the practical talk of routine work.

There is another facet to floor staff's conception of death as it applies to patients and residents at Murray Manor. Floor staff's death talk does not vary solely by what it considers differences in clientele sensibilities. It also is indirectly linked to floor staff's believed greater vulnerability to more alert clientele. Aides will not only say, "It's not good to talk about death in front of the more alert ones," but will add, "If they got frightened, it would just make your work that much harder." Floor aides feel that if they take into consideration the differences among patients and residents in their believed sensitivity to death, routine work with them is likely to be smoother than if they do not. The definitional precaution that aides take in not talking about death with "alert" patients or residents is a partial outcome of their general concern for maintaining normal floor routine.

Top staff's rare presence on the floors alters floor staff's death world. Floor aides make obvious efforts to whisper death talk and to conceal bed-and-body work on the deceased in the presence of patients who are believed to be senile as well as those considered alert. Floor staff's accountability to its superiors makes death a special event in their presence. This results from floor staff's perception of how top staff views death. Based on the directives it receives from top staff members when deaths occur and how they behave in death situations, floor staff believes that it is expected to act differently when a death occurs than otherwise. As an LPN on the fourth floor stated:

> When someone dies, Miss Timmons [director of nursing] calls up to get all the patients out of the halls and into their rooms. We're supposed to close all the doors. So everyone runs around getting patients into their rooms. Some of the patients get mad because they don't want to be shoved around. Of course, I have to do my job. Up here, I don't think that death frightens the other old people. I don't push my opinion too much because they'd think I don't care about the other patients or that I was morbid.

Floor staff's treatment of death as a special event tends to disappear as top staff members leave the death scene, however. In a situation where there are only so-called senile patients present along the floor and top staff personnel, there is a considerable amount of whispering in an atmosphere that is cautious and solemn.[3] As soon as it is known that top staff has left, death talk and bed-and-body work on the deceased become clear and obvious.

## Top Staff

Like the floor staff, persons occupying top staff roles do not experience dying or death. But, in contrast to floor staff, they are comparatively fleeting witnesses to both. When top staff witnesses dying, it is a relatively momentary and residual aspect of its administrative work. When it witnesses death, top staff mostly presides over it; that is, it appears on patient floors and directs floor staff in the variety of tasks associated with preparing a deceased person in a nursing home for the mortician. Its presence on the floors involves a rather solemn performance. When it presides, all floor behavior (both that of clientele and floor staff) is scrutinized for decorum, solemnity, and quiet urgency. Floor staff is very sensitive to this scrutiny. It changes floor staff's definition of death from being a routine part of work to being special.

On their relatively infrequent appearances on the floors when no death has occurred, top staff personnel talk mostly about the variety of administrative tasks in which they are involved. Their talk ranges from the progress of the patient census to comments about the physical appearance of the floors (odors, fire exits blocked, ashtrays found in nonsmoking areas, and so forth). When top staff members encounter patients who greet them, their response is standard, glib, and patronizing.

In the event of a death, when top staff appears on the floors, its talk contrasts dramatically with the foregoing. It may be highly patient-oriented and manipulative. Any patients who are encountered are conversationally indulged. Responses to patients' statements about their health are inquisitive and conciliatory. Efforts are made by the top staff to keep the topic of conversation away from death. As a matter of fact, while such talk proceeds, top staff members tend to lead patients away from the death scene.

Top staff's patient-oriented talk in a death scene does not vary with nursing home definitions of the alertness of patients. Regardless of how alert a patient is considered to be, top staff converses with him. This occurs even if a member of the top staff has to supply the entire content of talk with a patient. Top staff does not refer to or talk of death in the presence of any patients or residents, alert or otherwise. This stands in contrast to floor staff's definition of death talk as routine and open in the presence of those patients considered senile.

For top staff, the world of death in practice does not include dying. Dying is highly routine in the nursing home. It is considered a normal, taken-for-granted part of floor staff's work. Deaths, however, although they periodically occur, are conceived as special events. When a death occurs, and a member of the top staff is informed of it, he might typically say that he "will put his regular work aside for a while." After the body of the deceased has been adequately prepared and the death scene properly staged, I have heard top staff comment, "Well, I'll get back to my work since everything up here is under control." This, as well as other language, suggests that deaths are not conceived by top staff as part of the normal routine of dying in the nursing home. This conception of death, being separate from dying, generates its own special talk and behavior.

Death talk and behavior by top staff at the death scene differ from talk of death outside of it. Outside of the death scene, when top staff members were interviewed about dying and death in the nursing home, they tended not to separate the two conceptually. They typically said that they treated them both as "routine things." In response to top staff members' statements that they treated both dying and death as routine, they then were asked why, when there is a death at Murray Manor, everyone tends to act as if something special happened. Further, each person interviewed was reminded of the details of his solemn and indulgent performance at the death scene.

In every instance in which a member of the top staff was reminded of top staff behavior at death scenes, he or she would answer that what was being described was the old concept of protecting the living from the dead. Typical of these responses was a statement made by one of the administrative nurses:

> That stuff of protecting the patient is a bunch of old horseshit. Patients don't react. When everyone starts running around closing doors, that's when they get an idea that something must have happened. The new idea is to just try and be as natural as possible. I feel that that's the best thing.

Running through top staff's responses to questions on the treatment of death in the nursing home were references to the current conception of death in the nursing profession. Two top staff nurses cited examples from the various geriatric and nursing journals to which they subscribed about the need to "treat death as a normal and routine part of health care." They made mention of various books which they had read, the most popular of which was one by Kübler-Ross (1969), which advocates the normal and open treatment of dying and death.

It is evident that top staff's conception of dying and death is one thing in the context of the floor and another in situations where it speaks as self-defined geriatric professionals about the care of terminal patients. In the first instance, in its relations with staff and patients on the floors, top staff treats dying as separate from the event of death. When a death occurs and top staff presides over the death scene, the situation is not considered to be genuinely part of its usual work. In the second case, its reading of professional literature informs it that these events should not be separated but, rather, are to be considered and treated as normal and integral parts of the last stages of life.

## DEATH WORK

The worlds of main events are as variable as the socially structured viewpoints in their setting. Specific complexes of roles generate particular definitions of dying and death in the nursing home. Such definitions, however, do not simply emerge and continue as ongoing components of social life. They are sustained or suffer distortion and incredulity as a result of the work that persons do who occupy various positions in the setting. This work may be supported or hindered by the physical arrangements available to them.

### Death News

News of death is good or bad news, depending on the death world involved. Differences in definitions of death between clientele and top staff suggest separate orientations to death news. Patients and residents desire to be informed of deaths that occur in the home. In practice, top staff tries to contain death news because it believes such information is frightening to patients and residents. Floor staff works to support top staff's containment, partially because the latter is floor staff's superior and partially because floor staff believes that its routine work might become disrupted and difficult otherwise.

Floor and top staff attempt to contain death news in a variety of ways. When floor personnel discover that a patient might have died, they are required to page one of the top staff nurses immediately. The public address system is audible to everyone in the nursing home, both to staff and clientele on every floor simultaneously. When the floor staff pages a top staff nurse after a patient is thought to have died, it never announces the purpose of the call. Rather, a top staff nurse is told to come to the specific floor of the death.

The manner in which pages for death confirmations are made differs from pages for other matters. Their relative urgency differs. Death pages tend to be less casual than others. Also, death pages "command" the presence of a superior on the floor while nondeath pages usually are made as requests. These differences, although neither announces news of death, are clues to death events.

Not only do various floor and top staff members initially learn of possible deaths through "concealed" death pages, but so do patients and residents. Whenever a regular page is made over the public address system, patients and residents usually will show little response and make no specific comments on the call. However, when the page "commands" a top staff nurse (and sometimes the administrator) to come to a particular floor, it is not uncommon for patients or residents to react in one of two ways. They may look up from what they are doing and show obvious signs of listening or scrutinizing their premises. Or, they may ask themselves or some indefinite other person around them, "I wonder what's happening?" This is the first stage in the spread of death news.

Although the processing of death officially requires only the presence of one top staff nurse, when she is called in the event of a death, other top staff members hear the page, suspect a death, and tend to converge on the death scene. When top staff personnel arrive, if a death has occurred, they begin to preside over the processing of the body. Members of the top staff, defining death as a special event, proceed to stage a quietly urgent and solemn scene.

Now, from the patient and resident point of view, it is extraordinary to find so much of the "top brass" around. In the routine, day-to-day work of patient care, they are rarely to be seen, especially the non-nursing top staff which includes the administrator, social worker, and chaplain. Moreover, all top staff personnel are indulgent of patients while keeping an obvious eye on the death scene. To patients and residents, this too is rather unusual.

This is the second stage in the spread of death news. What was only a suspicion of some special event is now confirmed with the presence of special participants. At this point, although patients and residents may not yet definitely know that a death has occurred, they are aware of the possibility. The spread of death news among patients and residents beyond this point is contingent on the physical location and social relations of patients and residents in the nursing home.

The higher the floor level at Murray Manor, the less ambulatory the clientele. Physically, this means that on an upper floor, patients are more likely to be in their own rooms than on a lower one. Should someone die, the likelihood of other persons encountering clues to it in the hallway or in other rooms is less upstairs than on the first floor. Besides ambulatory variations between floors, there are variations in clientele intelligibility. Residents converse with each other more extensively than do patients.

These two factors influence the degree to which a patient's or resident's physical location in the nursing home hinders his receipt of death news. Patients who are bedfast and have difficulty conversing are largely confined to their rooms. Unless someone enters their rooms and directly informs them that a death has occurred, they are not likely to know.[4] Patients and residents who are ambulatory and conversant are not bound by the physical constraints of their rooms. When a death occurs, they are likely to become carriers of death news.

Top staff has a much more difficult time containing news of death on the first floor than it does on three and four. As a matter of fact, residents usually know of deaths on their own floor before the floor staff. When a member of the floor staff is called by a resident who has discovered someone as having possibly died, the floor and top staff attempt to "take over and keep us away from the room." This irritates and angers some residents. They desire to know correctly whether or not someone died so that, as one resident said, "You can feel that the person is at peace and not suffering, and then we can send condolences."[5]

Staff takes advantage of a number of physical arrangements to contain the spread of death news. Among these are closing doors, pulling curtains, feigning routine patient treatment, and removing a body while patients or residents are dining. Patients and residents also take advantage of arrangements, but to obtain death news. Some of them are "specialists" in that they have direct access to certain arrangements that present accurate death clues. They are the vigilant keepers of these clues. For example, certain patients and residents who have rooms that overlook the ambulance ramp at the rear of the building keep their "eye," as they say, on "what's going on out there." Other residents and patients systematically frequent different floors for a variety of reasons, such as visiting wives, friends, or to obtain services. Such persons are strategic links in the diffusion of death news between floors. When such links weaken (as they had upon the death of two residents' wives mentioned above), death news becomes more easily contained on each floor.

## Hiding the Body

Whenever there is a death on a floor, the body of the deceased is washed and wrapped before it is considered ready to be taken out by morticians. In practice, top staff considers this to be a morbid affair for other patients to witness, or of which to be aware.

Until recently, whenever a patient died who had shared a room with someone, his body was discreetly removed from the room and placed in one that was empty. The body then was prepared in the empty room. In the process of moving the body, patients standing or walking in the hallway in the immediate vicinity were calmly urged toward the other end, the fire doors sometimes being closed after them.

At the present time, the patient census is often so high that all rooms on some currently open floor may be filled. When someone dies, there are no empty rooms available to prepare the body for the mortician. Staff has no private place to do its body work in the usual nonchalant, perfunctory way. Because of the lack of empty rooms, top staff believes that something must be done so that the body can be prepared without patients' becoming aware of it.

Responding to the problem of not having a private place for dealing with the deceased, top staff directs floor personnel to take advantage of the "normal" appearance of bed-and-body work by passing off the process of preparing the dead as treating the seriously ill. It is routine for nurses' aides to enter patients' rooms and give them bed baths. While doing this, they usually pull the curtain that separates patients sharing a single room. This normal routine also allows them to prepare the body. In the case of the deceased, they must not only bathe the body, but they must do so as if performing the usual bed-and-body work on living bedfast patients. For example, when a roommate is present on the other side of a pulled curtain and that roommate is believed to be "alert," aides preparing the body will not talk about the body in a depersonalized way, which would signify to the roommate that it is lifeless. The dead patient is adjusted (face and body posture) to make him appear as if sleeping. His eyes are closed, mouth shut, and his head is turned to one side. The appearance of the "sleeping" dead and the sleeping living are strikingly similar.

## Encounters with Dying

Whenever residents wish to use services that are located in the vicinity of dying patients, they proceed with caution. The beauty and barber shop is on the third floor. As residents proceed to get their hair set or cut, they will often comment, "It makes me nervous when I have to go up there." They'll typically add, "You never know what you'll see." This is generally followed by talk that expresses sympathy for the dying mixed with expressed feelings of depression.

When they enter the premises of those known to be dying, they become visibly wary. As soon as the elevator doors open onto floors that house dying patients, residents' eye movements peruse the premises in much more careful scrutiny than is typical for them in other situations in the nursing home. When the floor area immediately surrounding the elevator is considered to be adequately safe of the signs of dying, residents tend to proceed quickly to their destinations. Rarely do they continue to scrutinize the premises.

Residents who have friends on patient floors attempt to avoid visiting them there. They sometimes go so far as to fetch and accompany patient friends to the first floor to visit with them rather than the reverse. When they cannot do this, their visits are notably shorter, less frequent, and less comfortable. They sit in patient rooms or the parlors of patient floors with obvious apprehension. When someone who shows what they consider visible signs of dying (moaning, emaciation, odors of decay, and so forth) appears before them, they grimace or turn away.

Top staff does not usually take patients' sentiments about dying into consideration in making room assignments. In practice, it is certainly concerned that roommates do not witness death, but not so for dying. When patients believe that they are being unduly exposed to dying, they sometimes become quite vehement in requesting a change in the situation. They complain to the floor staff, they weep, and they may threaten to request their relatives to remove them from the nursing home as a last resort. When top staff receives these requests and threats, it typically interprets them as "unrealistic" demands that stem from not being "properly adjusted." To patients, this is not considered a problem of adjustment, but rather, an injustice.

## CONCLUSION

C. Wright Mills (1963) once said that much of what are popularly called "personal troubles" are not rooted in individual problems of character, but rather in the human impact of societal structures and institutions and of changes in them. It is suggested here that, in small worlds, another source of personal troubles is the differential conceptions of events that emerge out of varied, locally structured experiences. Insofar as persons are socially differentiated within face-to-face, organized settings, their acts and sentiments are influenced by the set of social definitions that exists in them. Persons' troubles are, to some extent, outcomes of the "reasonable" actions that follow from the various subworlds that share a common social setting. Troubles result from "reasonable" actions because there are multiple worlds of social logic, each internally "normal," but often considered irrational from without. Death worlds at Murray Manor are like this. They are definitions of main events that are constructed out of the experiences of persons who do not perceive dying and death from completely common circumstances. Murray Manor organizes varied definitions within a single setting. Persons' troubles in the nursing home in relationship to dying and death are an inevitable aspect of "living" together. These are, in effect, organized troubles.

## NOTES

1. In order to document these varied worlds of death, data were gathered during three months of daily observation of, and participation in, the routine work and life of staff and clientele in a nursing home—Murray Manor. (References to places and persons throughout are pseudonyms.) Nurses and aides were accompanied on a wide variety of patient rounds, ranging from the distribution of medications to such personal care as help in voiding and eating. Staff meetings were attended, both the informal, unscheduled meetings of floor personnel and the scheduled conferences of the top (administrative) staff. Staff also was observed in many nonwork situations, for example, at mealtimes, during breaks, and in informal chats throughout the day. My participation in the daily lives of clientele took many forms. They were visited, greeted, and accompanied. During regular visiting hours, I joined relatives in their rooms. Many chats—in halls, parlors, outdoors, dining rooms, bathrooms, and in physical therapy—took place. Clientele were accompanied (all as participants) at table, parties, chapel, dying, and death.

Initially, 55 formal interviews were conducted with the administrative staff and clientele. Nine of these were staff interviews. All of these persons were reinterviewed, both formally and informally, at various points throughout the study as the need arose. Specific research questions often necessitated recontacting particular kinds of persons, both staff and clientele, for data. Initial interviews were tape-recorded and transcribed. Later interview data were recorded as field notes.

2. The friendship variable affects the social organization of death by making death an interpersonal as well as public ending.

3. Whispering and solemnity are not simply an artifact of top staff presence, but rather of presence in a death scene. When top staff is present on the floor at other times, there is an obvious increase in cautiousness but no extensive whispering or solemnity.

4. There is an exception to this. Patients who have difficulty conversing are often labeled "senile" by floor staff. Aides will readily talk about bed-and-body work on the deceased in their presence, assuming they are not alert to the content of talk. Close attention to such patients' speech indicates that they often are aware of death in such circumstances, though they tend not to spread death news.

5. At one time, residents were very angry at being the victims of a false rumor about one of them who had "died" while at the hospital. As soon as they heard of the "death," they all eulogized and began the process of socially closing the life of the "deceased." When they realized it was a false rumor, they had to reconstruct their sentiments. Some felt that they had been made fools.

# REFERENCES

BERGER, P. L. and T. LUCKMANN (1966) The Social Construction of Reality. New York: Doubleday.

BLUMER, H. (1969) Symbolic Interactionism. Englewood Cliffs, N.J.: Prentice-Hall.

DOUGLAS, J. (1973) Introduction to Sociology: Situations and Structures. New York: Free Press.

GLASER, B. G. and A. STRAUSS (1965) Awareness of Dying. Chicago: Aldine.

GOFFMAN, E. (1971) Relations in Public. New York: Harper & Row.

KUBLER-ROSS, E. (1969) On Death and Dying. New York: Macmillan.

MILLS, C. W. (1963) Power, Politics and People. New York: Ballantine.

THOMAS, W. I. (1966) On Social Organization and Social Personality (M. Janowitz, ed.). Chicago: Univ. of Chicago Press.

*SARAH MATTHEWS* is a Ph.D. candidate in sociology at the University of California, Davis. She is completing a doctoral dissertation on social-psychological aspects of being old.

# OLD WOMEN AND

# IDENTITY MAINTENANCE:

*Outwitting the Grim Reaper*

## SARAH MATTHEWS

**A** BASIC TENET of symbolic interactionism is that homo sapiens in the process of becoming human gain self-consciousness by taking the attitudes of others toward their own bodies, actions, and thoughts. Biological humans become persons and have selves when they are able to see themselves as both the subject and object of situations. In Mead's terms, they possess a self composed of the "I," the participant in each moment of the day, and the "me," the attitudes of others adopted to preview and judge their own participation (Mead, 1970: 135-226). In preparing to act, humans mentally rehearse actions to assess the possible meanings and gauge others' reactions to them in order to project and maintain the image they have of themselves (Goffman, 1959).

In most situations, persons are engaged in the process of ascertaining the symbolic significance of their actions to themselves and others. In situations which have not been accomplished, which are in the planning stage, the participating self, the "I," cannot be known absolutely. Persons plan for future acts, but "the real self that appears in that act awaits the completion of the act itself" (Mead, 1970: 203). Even so, most persons are able to plan for the future with reasonable confidence and, except in stressful situations, rarely question their ability to maintain a personally acceptable self-image.[1]

For old persons the prospect of physical and mental infirmity, dependence, and death looms ever larger with each passing year, making problematic their ability to project and maintain a desired self-image in the future.[2] The actual dying process, with all its unknowns, may mean that the old person will be in situations in which s/he will be a participant and at the same time be unable to participate in negotiating the definitions of those situations. For this person there will be no "signs given," only "signs given off" (Goffman, 1959: 2); and these will be signs over which the dying (or dead) participant has little or no control.

Old persons, then, are faced with the possibility in the unknowable future (and in the knowable future, since death is inevitable), of situations in which they will be unable to present themselves as the persons they "really are," situations in which projecting their own views of themselves, their self-identities, may be out of their control.[3] This is the problematic situation addressed in the analysis that follows. The basic uncertainty of the how and when of death is a recurrent topic among old women.[4] This concept of uncertainty will be presented first, followed by a discussion of the strategies employed to eliminate the uncertainty and maintain a desired self-identity in dying and death.[5]

## DEATH AND UNCERTAINTY

That death cannot be definitively planned for is mentioned often by old people in a variety of ways. For example, one old woman told of a birthday party for another woman in her sewing club:

And you know, that night that woman passed away. Died in her sleep. We were all just sick about it. She had been quite well for the last few years. She'd had heart trouble. The next day one of her friends called to tell me and I said, "Why I can't believe it!" I remember the last thing she said. She came over to where I was sewing and said goodbye. We had had such a wonderful lunch. We had a beautiful cake for her. Honestly, you know, we're here today and gone tomorrow.

Another old woman pointed out that there is no logic that will predict time of death, even when it appears that there might be.

There's another widow up here. Her husband was at the prison for years and he retired. And they were both kind of sickly, but she was more sickly than he, and yet he passed away and she's still here. You never know, do you? He seemed like to go so sudden.

One informant explained to the interviewer:

That's what I say about your mother. You don't know what will happen. You don't know. You can't live but today. Yesterday's gone, and tomorrow's hearsay. You don't know what will happen to your mother. She may die overnight with a heart attack and she may live to be 103. You don't know.

Other references to the uncertainty with which old people are faced is evident in conversations such as the following.

First of July, if I live, first of July I was married 65 years.

If anything happens to me [before the trip] you'll give the money to my son, won't you? We never know what might happen. You'll read about it in the paper. You'll know if something happens to me.

I haven't been to Las Vegas since my oldest boy was two years old. I'm going to go next year. [slight pause] If I'm still here.

I want to live to go see him when he's 90.

When death will occur, then, cannot be predicted and, therefore, cannot be taken into account when planning for the future. One old woman summed up her thoughts on death in a statement that is representative of old women generally: "Why should I worry about that? It's something everybody has to accept, but I'm not looking forward to it."

Death may be taken as inevitable and not worth worrying about, but the process of dying is another matter entirely. The events that will precede death, again, cannot be predicted, but old women can plan in order to maintain their self-identities during the dying process. Fear of the dying process centers on "suffering" and "being a burden," both of which fall under the category of losing control over self-identity.

> I'm not in a hurry to die because I feel like I've still got quite a bit to accomplish here. I'm not afraid of death itself, but I'm afraid of pain. I have a fear of lingering. That I don't want to do. I don't want to have to be taken care of. I've been active all my life and taken care of myself and I just don't want anybody to have to take care of me. Not a fear of death, but a fear of being probably in a wheelchair and having a stroke and having to lie in bed or in a rest home.

There are various strategies that the old woman uses to control self-identity during the dying process. She, of course, cannot be certain that she will be able to maintain control over her self and social identities, but she may use strategies that make potential loss of control less uncertain.

## MONITORING WARNING SIGNALS

For the old woman a visit to the doctor takes on new meaning: it becomes a safeguard against lingering. The strategy here is to watch carefully the signs that are associated with a long dying process, and thereby avoid one. One old woman goes to her doctor regularly even though she is in "pretty good shape."

> I do go for checkups and high blood pressure, you know. You've got to watch that when you get over 70. You watch because that's the time when you're more likely to have a stroke or something like that. That's one thing I have a screaming horror of, is being disabled and lay around for years disabled. But that's God's will. We can't say, but I do watch my blood pressure on account of that my mother-in-law died of a stroke, my father-in-law died of a stroke, and we'll say indirectly my husband died of a stroke. And I know what it's all about. If they had watched their blood pressure and their diet when they found out it was high. . . .

Other activities are also performed as a way of increasing the likelihood that lingering can be avoided. One informant forced herself to take a daily walk in order to avoid being crippled by arthritis. Another woman said that she had played bridge three days in succession and gone to a church meeting the day before, so she was "laying off for the rest of the week to balance it off," to avoid a heart attack. She had had one twelve years earlier.

There appears to be a belief held by old women that if they monitor their bodies very carefully, they will increase the probability of living longer than otherwise, and that when they die, they will go quickly.

## SYMBOLIC MAINTENANCE OF SELF-IDENTITY

Planning in advance for the division of property and for funeral arrangements is another way to maintain self-identity while dying and dead. Possessions that are valuable to the old woman may be viewed as "ego-involvements" (Shibutani, 1961: 224), in that they become experienced as part of the old woman herself, and as such can be used symbolically in interaction with others. She can plan a distribution of her possessions so that everyone who is important to her knows how she feels about him or her, even when she no longer has control over her self-identity. The concern with who gets what, then, appears to be not so much a concern with living on in possessions after death, as is often assumed, but with maintaining, when no longer in control, an image of self that is acceptable. For example, one old woman said, "I hate to leave little Christy [granddaughter]. That [china] is all for Christy after I've gone." The same goal is attained in distributing goods while she is still of sound mind and body. "I've given all my good things and dishes to my granddaughter. I dearly love her." Another informant was in the process of carefully making a list of her possessions and dividing them equitably between her two granddaughters. Her concern was not so much that her possessions have good homes, but that her relatives see her as fair and benevolent. Thus, by planning very carefully in advance, she felt she would be maintaining her image of herself even when she would no longer be here.

One old woman wished to convey a very different message to her relatives. In commenting on her practice of sending her grandson five dollars every Saturday, she said, "That way, when the vultures come around, there won't be anything left." The following description of how another old woman plans her funeral suggests the message she is sending to her daughter with whom she has a less-than-ideal relationship.

> I've joined that Memorial thing and I'm just going to fix it so that they come over and pack me up and take me over and cremate me. For years I hated the idea of cremation. It seemed so unnatural. Putting your body back in the earth and letting it do what it could to feed back seemed more natural. Since I'm old, it would just seem sensible to get it over in 24 hours. The first time this happened to my friends, it just seemed monstrous to me, to take a body that was still warm and put it in the crematorium. But after all, what does it matter? Just save her [daughter] having to make a decision. And it's expensive. . . . Why go to the expense? Burials have become so expensive. Fifteen hundred dollars to plant a body is kind of ridiculous today. I realized after my mother died, and I wished I'd realized it before. If you're going to give flowers to people, do it while they can still smell them. The time to say I love you is when they can still respond, because there is no response in a dead body. She will do what she pleases. I think my daughter is motivated by a lot of fear. I think my daughter is scared to death of an awful lot of things.[6]

By planning for an impersonal cremation, this old woman will be symbolically interacting with her "irresponsible" daughter, using the disposition of her body to maintain her own view of herself and her daughter in the distressing relationship. Most incidents of this strategy are less overt and are found in such statements as, "My children know what I want. . . ." Thus, the old woman designates others to maintain her self-image when it is no longer in her control.

## *PLANNING FOR SUDDEN PHYSICAL MALFUNCTION*

One constant source of uncertainty for the old woman is not knowing when or where her body will fail her. The fear of being completely helpless and no one being aware of the fact is voiced often.[7] For example: "I don't know what I would do in the night, if I were to have a stroke or something and couldn't get to the telephone." She deals with this potential dilemma by making arrangements with a neighbor on the other side of the wall. "All I have to do is knock." Or as another informant explained,

> What worries me is when you live alone, and when you get older, you don't know when death will strike. You might be alone, might have sort of a heart attack when you're alone, and you could be alone for two or three days before anyone would know. That's the part that bothers me. Anne always calls me up at nine in the morning and I always manage to be here so I won't worry her. I'm quite sure that if I didn't answer and she tried and tried. . . . We have a sort of plan like that.

The image of herself suffering and being unable to call for help is frightening, but the image of herself being dead and no one taking note of her passing is also frightening and threatening to her sense of self. By carefully arranging her daily rounds, she is able to minimize the possibility of being in a completely helpless condition or dead for a long period of time without anyone knowing.

Another old woman is fearful of where her body will suddenly fail her.

> Every time I go out on the street, I think of this—if I should collapse. In this city I don't know anybody anymore. I used to know about everybody who lived here years and years ago. Now I don't know anybody and they don't know me. And I always think—if I should collapse. I have a horror of that medical center out there. I have a horror of that place. The County Hospital it used to be. And I think, if I should collapse, that's where they'll cart me, out there, and I have such a horror of it. I think about that a lot.

She deals with this uncertainty by carrying a card with her that has her doctor's name on it, "So that might help." Like other old people, this woman lives with the fear that she will suddenly become a body to be "carted" instead of the "person" she is.

One atypical old woman confronts the uncertainty surrounding the dying process by adopting an ideology that eliminates uncertainty.

> I think probably as you grow older your will to survive is not so great. . . . I think there ought to be euthanasia. Is there any point to lingering on until you are totally incapacitated? What's so wonderful about life? It's the quality of life, not the quantity. I would much rather choose to die than to live with cancer or stroke or heart condition.

And in "choosing" she will eliminate potential lack of control over her self-identity.

For the old woman, the unknowable circumstances surrounding a potential malfunction of the body are taken into account and planned for so that their effect on her self and social identities may be minimized and at least some of the felt precariousness of her situation diminished.

## CONCLUSION

Ignoring the work of the Grim Reaper becomes increasingly difficult as one year makes way for the next and gradually lengthens each person's accumulated time on earth. For old persons, death, and the period of time preceding it, come inevitably closer, and the prospect of being physically dependent on someone and of no longer being an active participant in social life become possibilities that are taken into account. This analysis has dealt with a number of ways in which old women attempt to make the dying process less uncertain, with fewer ambiguities that might be interpreted inaccurately and be damaging to the self-images they wish to project.

Death itself is faced with resignation.[8] One old woman summed up the situation, "I guess everybody's life is different and you just have to live on until you're taken. There's nothing you can do about it." At the same time, death and the dying process are not seen as the end of the self, but as situations requiring careful planning to maintain the person that the old woman sees herself to be. The women who supplied the data for this analysis would agree with Simone de Beauvoir (1972: 441) as she contemplates her own death.

> I shall be dead for others, not for myself: it is the Other who is mortal in my being. I know that I am mortal, just as I know that I am old, by adopting the outsider's view of me. This knowledge is therefore abstract, general, and assumed from without. My "mortality" is in no way the object of any close, inward experience. I am not unaware of it; in practical life I take it into account in my plans and my decisions, in so far as I treat myself as an Other: but I do not *feel* it.

## NOTES

1. See Messinger et al. (1968) for a discussion of the problems faced by persons whose views of themselves are felt to be problematic in all situations. For most of us in most situations, our images of ourselves are taken for granted.

2. At this point in history in this society, death is something that "naturally" happens to old persons: "Whatever the complex problems of the roles this group of 'oldsters' are to assume, or have already assumed, they are a group who, by the nature of their position in the society, are 'living in the shadow of death,' since they have entered what is by all institutional criteria, a terminal period of their lives" (Parsons, 1963: 62).

3. The concept of self-identity is used here to refer to the way persons view themselves. Goffman (1963: 105) chooses to call this "ego identity," defined as a person's "subjective sense of his own situation and of his own continuity and character that an individual comes to obtain as a result of various social experiences." McCall and Simmons (1966: 67) use "role-identity" in the same way to refer to an individual's "imaginative view of himself *as he likes to think of himself being and acting* as an occupant of that position."

4. Although death is often considered a "taboo topic" by sociologists and Cowgill (1972) and Cumming and Henry (1961: 63) found that only a tiny fraction of their samples admitted thinking about death and dying, Hochschild (1973: 79) in a participant observation study of a senior citizens' housing project found that death "was a fact of life in Merrill Court and there was no taboo against talking about it."

5. The data on which this analysis is based are conversations in which at least one of the participants is a widowed woman aged 65 or over. The data were gathered over a period of 14 months through participant observation in various settings including a senior citizens' center in which the author was employed for seven months, public

housing projects for the elderly, and other informal situations; through 22 "hired hand" interviews in which the author trained 5 interviewers to conduct tape recorded guided conversations with widows over 70 with children who had applied, sometimes successfully, for public housing; and through 5 intensive interviews conducted by the author.

6. This informant's discussion of her corpse is unusual. Hochschild (1973: 84-85) found that, "Although the widows talked about the events leading up to death and death itself frankly, in detail, and even in a matter-of-fact way, they seldom mentioned what happened to the body afterward. It is as if the taboo that for young people stops before death, is for old people moved beyond it. . . . Although death was not considered depressing, the use of one's physical remains was."

7. The informants who furnished the data for this analysis are all widows living alone. Old women who live with spouses, in households with older people, or in apartments or houses equipped with emergency call buttons and lights may not see sudden physical malfunctions as problematic. Unfortunately, the resolution of this issue lies outside the scope of these data.

8. Becker (1962: 70) writes most eloquently of the resignation with which death is faced. "The self is a symbolic fiction which throbs with experiences that mere flesh and blood could never relay. The self trails its body into old age, after a lifetime of daily scrutiny in a mirror, of a biological aging process it does not understand. Approaching death, the magnificent, intricate, symbolic creation of history—the self—can show only resignation. For the self-reflexive animal, death is an absurd injustice, which thousands of years and unnumbered systems of thought have labored to explain."

## REFERENCES

BECKER, E. (1962) The Birth and Death of Meaning. New York: Free Press.

COWGILL, D. O. (1972) "Aging in American society," pp. 243-261 in D. O. Cowgill and L. D. Holmes (eds.) Aging and Modernization. New York: Appleton-Century-Crofts.

CUMMING, E. and W. E. HENRY (1961) Growing Old. New York: Basic Books.

de BEAUVOIR, S. (1972) The Coming of Age. New York: G. F. Putnam's Sons.

GOFFMAN, E. (1963) Stigma: Notes on the Management of Spoiled Identity. Englewood Cliffs, N.J.: Prentice-Hall.

——— (1959) Presentation of Self in Everyday Life. Garden City, N.Y.: Doubleday-Anchor.

HOCHSCHILD, A. R. (1973) The Unexpected Community. Englewood Cliffs, N.J.: Prentice-Hall.

McCALL, G. J. and J. L. SIMMONS (1966) Identities and Interactions. New York: Free Press.

MEAD, G. H. (1970) Mind, Self, and Society. Chicago: Univ. of Chicago Press.

MESSINGER, S. L., H. SAMPSON, and R. D. TOWNE (1968) "Life as theater: some notes on the dramaturgic approach to social reality," pp. 7-18 in M. Truzzi (ed.) Sociology and Everyday Life. Englewood Cliffs, N.J.: Prentice-Hall.

PARSONS, T. (1963) "Death in American society—a brief working paper." Amer. Behavioral Scientist 6 (May): 61-65.

SHIBUTANI, T. (1961) Society and Personality: An Interactionist Approach to

*VICTOR W. MARSHALL* is Assistant Professor in the Department of Sociology at McMaster University, Hamilton, Ontario. He is involved in a study of professional socialization of medical students, in a study of teamwork on hospital wards, and in further theorizing about aging and dying as status passage.

# ORGANIZATIONAL FEATURES OF
# TERMINAL STATUS PASSAGE IN
# RESIDENTIAL FACILITIES FOR THE AGED

## VICTOR W. MARSHALL

**D**YING MAY BE VIEWED sociologically as a career involving a passagee (the dying person) and, in some cases, others who accompany him or who control aspects of his status passage. In this paper, I focus on a home for the aged (St. Joseph's) and a retirement village (Glen Brae) as representative communities of the aging and dying. The two settings are viewed as sociocultural milieux in which residents live and, potentially, at least, participate in constructing the status passage reality wherein their own dying occurs. This reality includes the organization of their dying careers—involving the development of views of career termination—as well as other aspects of their lives as aging and dying people.

A number of observers have suggested that the extent to which the lives of elderly residents of congregate housing are generally satisfactory is greatly influenced by the degree of

*AUTHOR'S NOTE:* I am indebted to the residents and administration of the two settings described here, to the Canada Council and McMaster University for research support, and to Berkeley Fleming for valuable comments on earlier drafts.

[115]

independence and resident-initiated organization (Aldridge, 1956; Kalson, 1972; Messer, 1967; Seguin, 1973). My restricted concern here is with the relationship between organizational features and the development among aged individuals of a sense that their dying status passage is appropriate or legitimate. The analysis focuses first on the differing structuring of time and then on the characteristics of the dying career within the two settings. As we shall see, the two communities are widely disparate in terms of their characteristic patternings of living and dying. Comparing them provides an opportunity to theorize about the influence of organizational features of residential settings for the aging on the degree to which and the ways in which passagees construct and legitimize their own dying and deaths.

Data used in this analysis stem from field research supplemented by interviewing in the two settings. Glen Brae is a rambling, modern, 300-apartment structure housing about 400 residents in a campus-like setting in a suburban environment in the eastern United States. Residents purchase their apartments on a "life-care" principle which includes transfer to an attached nursing-care facility should this become necessary. Fully 78% of the residents are female, but only 15% of females are married. About half the females are widowed, and just under a third have never married. Three-fourths of the males are still living with their spouses, the remainder being widowed. These sex and marital-status imbalances are not highly irregular, given the average age of the residents (80) and the age range (64 to 96). As in most similar communities, residents are educationally privileged, with less than one-fifth having no more than a high school education. Religious adherence is mixed, but largely Protestant. The community has been described more extensively elsewhere (Marshall, 1973, 1975).

St. Joseph's, located 20 miles from the retirement village, provides a marked contrast. A decaying red-brick structure in a suburban area, it houses approximately 70 people, plus 45 on a fully integrated nursing floor. The age range, 64 to 98, is comparable to that at Glen Brae. About 80% of the residents are supported through welfare. As at Glen Brae, the residents are primarily female. None, however, live with their spouses. Those able to pay their own way have private rooms; the majority live in dormitories. The infirmary, located on the main floor, houses those in need of more intensive care. A registered nurse is on duty at all times. A minority of residents, because of ethnic background, speak English with difficulty or not at all. All residents are nominally Catholic, and the home is administered by nuns.

## TEMPORAL STRUCTURING OF ACTIVITIES

The timing of life in any organized setting depends on the synchronization, sequencing, and frequency of activities as well as on the activities themselves.[1] St. Joseph's Home and Glen Brae present vivid contrasts on the temporal structuring of activities.

At St. Joseph's, as in other relatively "total" institutions (Goffman, 1961: 6), virtually all aspects of life are carried out in the company of others treated in the same way. Activities are, for the most part, regularly sequenced but infrequent. The pace of life is slow. Meals exemplify the important events of the day because, on the typical day, nothing else happens. A bell beckons the residents to preassigned tables of six which are sex-segregated and unchanging. There is little conversation (due perhaps to language differences and to the lack of variety in table mates). Within 15 minutes, most of the residents have left the dining room. There are no planned daily activity programs.[2] The Directress is aware of the practice in similar institutions of encouraging residents to participate in planned activities but she thinks it preferable to leave them alone. About mid-morning, three or four residents might be found helping some of the Sisters with sewing and mending. A mid-day walk through the dormitories finds more than half the residents lying on top of their freshly made beds. Other activities are limited to the use of a few television lounges and sunporches and a basement recreation room where the men go for a smoke in the evening, generally sitting in silence. Conversation or any other activity in this room is infrequent—so much so that it took me about three weeks to work up the nerve to venture into it.

There is a monthly party, a birthday celebration for those having a birthday during the period. And the auxiliary does run a monthly bingo game. Yet residents are primarily spectators at these events. During bingo, for example, a volunteer stands over each player and when the number is called, moves the tab on the card.[3] The only event of note which truly breaks routine—a summer bus trip to a beach organized by the administration— does so only because its routine is on a once-yearly basis. In fact, the temporal structuring at St. Joseph's is so routinized and so slow that serious illness and death and its accompanying funeral (see below) become, ironically, the major novelties which interrupt the sameness of daily living. (See Gustafson, 1972, for a similar finding.) My field work at St. Joseph's was intermittent and thus, as a matter of course, I would ask upon my return, "What's new?" Although no one knew that death and dying were of particular interest to me, I was invariably told that what was new was that a death had occurred.

The situation at Glen Brae is a study in contrasts. Meals, for example, are anything but lock-step occasions. Residents may eat in their own kitchen-equipped apartments, in a snack bar, or in the dining room during extensive serving hours (evening meals in the dining room are part of the rental package). Seating arrangements are a matter of choice, and a hostess will introduce newcomers or isolates to those with whom they may wish to share a table. Table size varies and this, together with the freedom to choose one's partners, leads to broad-ranging and extensive informal interaction. Dining is frequently pre- ceded by small cocktail parties in the apartments, but whether any of these are scheduled or not, the walk to and from meals is customarily made in company.

Like dining arrangements, recreational pursuits are flexible and provide resident-initiated and planned possibilities for interaction with others. Throughout the day, depending on season, one sees the residents busy at lawn-bowls, shuffleboard, swimming, bridge games in the many lounges, or tending small flower gardens outside their apartments. There is a wide variety of scheduled and nonscheduled events, none of which are organized by the administration. A resident-initiated and run house government—the Forum—plans and implements a range of concerts, movies, lectures, religious services, craft and hobby groups, hiking trips, and field trips to neighboring cultural and recreational affairs. The Forum itself, with its many committees, is another source of activity and involvement. Residents produce their own newspaper, run their own library, and field their own choral group. The contrast with St. Joseph's was symbolized for me on the first visit I made to each setting shortly before Christmas: at St. Joseph's, the nuns were putting up Christmas decorations; at Glen Brae, residents were making their own.

In sum, while in neither setting does the administration formally encourage activity, time is structured very differently within each. At St. Joseph's the routine is repetitious, slow-paced, and lacking in novelty. When activities are scheduled, they are rarely done so at the initiative of residents. As one St. Joseph's resident noted, when asked how far ahead he planned, "I really don't, because it's all planned for you here. It's all routine." Asked if he missed that [planning], he said, "I did, but not any more." At Glen Brae, in contrast, the swift pace of activities is initiated by residents who in turn can draw upon them to piece together a day that breaks routine. Even the low activity level of a small minority of Glen Brae residents is higher than that of the most active person at St. Joseph's. I met no resident at St. Joseph's who kept a daily personal calendar, but I seldom met anyone at Glen Brae who did not. I did not have to schedule appointments for interviews at St. Joseph's, but I found it necessary to do so at Glen Brae. The slow pace of St. Joseph's resulted in death being highlighted, whereas the busy round of life at Glen Brae tended to dilute the vivid presence of death. The active involvements of residents in fashioning a way of life at Glen Brae provided, as we shall see, an interactional substratum for dealing with death such as was not developed at St. Joseph's.

## THE DYING CAREER

A move to either Glen Brae or St. Joseph's is, virtually for all, the final move. When one of the St. Joseph's residents died unexpectedly, I was told by another. "That's fifteen in five months." Total deaths the year before had been 20, and just 16 the year before that, for rates of approximately 17 and 14%.[4] All but two had occurred in the home. St. Joseph's is a place where people go to die; and the residents know it. As the resident who kept a tally put it,

> I knew what the home was for. In fact the day I moved in here they had a death. Now for the past three years I write them down. Just for curiosity to keep a law of averages.

Glen Brae is also a place where people go to die and know it. The move to the retirement village heightens awareness of finitude. Considerable financial resources must be expended under the life-care provision, and a commitment is made to pay monthly rental fees until death. Intendedly rational decision-making thus involves, for all except the very rich, an estimate of just what the cost will be over that period before death, and this necessitates some estimate of life expectancy (discussed at length in Marshall, 1973). As one resident described this bargain, "They come here to die, you know, to spend their last days. . . . It's a form of insurance to come here—based on life expectancy."

Both settings, then, are recognized by the residents as places to die. But the impact of this recognition differs because of the differing ways in which dying careers within them are organized.

## Dying at St. Joseph's

Dying is a social event; people die in the context of others who define their dying. Glaser and Strauss (1968: 6) use the term "dying trajectory" to refer to an individual's socially defined course of dying. As socially perceived, the dimensions of dying

> depend on when the perceiver initially *defines* someone as dying and on his expectations of how that dying will proceed. Dying trajectories themselves, then, are perceived courses of dying rather than their actual courses.

In this respect, we may note with Sudnow (1967: 62) that

> the characteristics "he is dead" and "he is dying" . . . are the products of assessment procedures, i.e., constitute the outcomes of investigative inquiries of more or less detail, undertaken by persons more or less practically involved in the consequences that discovery of those outcomes foreseeably have.

At St. Joseph's, the term "dying" tends to be reserved for the very last stages. As one aide noted, "When they start dying, they don't last for but a day. Some of them take longer." As such, while the residents may be "socially dead" (Kalish, 1968; Gustafson, 1972) to the outside world, they at least begin their residence in the home defined by staff as alive. The trajectory towards death begins, rather, with a definition of the resident as seriously ill or as needing intensive care. This leads to a move from the dormitory or private room on the second or third floor to the main infirmary floor. Then, if or when the prognosis of "dying" is made, the resident is moved to a special room, called at times the "dying room," but known to both staff and residents as "St. Peter's Room" (not a pseudonym), which, ironically, is room 13. At times there is a waiting list for this room, as my field notes record: "Sally and another aide said there are three people just waiting to die. So one is in St. Peter's Room. The other two are still in their own rooms." The dying trajectory implications of the room are appreciated with great clarity by the residents. One man, for example, who was placed in St. Peter's Room with a "dying" prognosis, got up in the middle of the night and made his way back to his own room.

Through St. Peter's Room, the dying of St. Joseph's residents is symbolically marked off from their living. But ritual, coupled with the fact that death is not disguised, keeps death in a prominent place in the minds of residents. The bodies of the dead were swiftly removed by a mortician, but invariably returned for the public funeral—a ritual which, because of the frequency of its occurrence, must have been important in the lives of the residents. These funerals were the prerogative of a single priest who had very definite ideas as to their ritual value. All dead received the same funeral mass (which, since it replaced the regular daily mass, always received a good turnout). During it, a "respectable" representation of the ambulatory would listen to a lengthy sermon emphasizing the love and mercy of God, the importance of leading a good life, and the privilege of being able to pray for the soul of a community member. When giving his funeral sermon, the priest used a booming voice which could be heard throughout the building, even down on the basement floor, two stories below. This, he indicated, was quite intentional. He wished to be heard both by those residents who were hard of hearing and also by those who had *not* come to the chapel. At the end of the services, the open coffin would be wheeled to the foot of the chapel, the residents would file past, hesitate briefly and then go out to view the funeral procession leaving the grounds.

This is routine in a setting where 15 to 20 funerals are held each year. On the day of one funeral, a birthday party was held in the afternoon. No references to the funeral were made as the residents enjoyed the festivities marking off an additional year's passage toward the same fate.

In summary, St. Joseph's Home is a place where people go to die, where an important aspect of daily life centers around the fact that people die there, and where death receives considerable ritual treatment. What is noteworthy about St. Joseph's, as a community where people die, is that dying is organized *for* the residents, not *by* them.

## Dying at Glen Brae

As I have discussed the organizational features of dying at Glen Brae at some length elsewhere (Marshall, 1975), I will here only briefly note those features which contrast with the situation at St. Joseph's.

The administration had no formal policy or plans concerning the management of dying and death as a community event, but early on in the history of the village, residents began to organize and to develop informal means of dealing with death. A retired psychologist living in Glen Brae suggested that management avoid euphemisms in referring to the death of a resident, and that simple obituary notices be posted when someone died. By the time the community had been in existence for a little over a year, an editorial written by the head of the Forum appeared in the resident newspaper. It referred to a rising death rate, and urged residents to adopt a determination to "look toward the future and be prepared. . . . It is up to us, not management, to make Glen Brae the haven we desire." Residents were urged not to make vivid displays of grief. Death, then, was to be treated informally and discreetly at Glen Brae; but it was not to be ignored.

As at St. Joseph's, the definition of a resident as dying has interactional consequences. At some point the dying of a resident will lead to his removal to the extended care facility, which is somewhat separated from the residential section, though accessible by an enclosed corridor. This provision serves the function of effectively removing the vivid presence of death from the midst of the community (Friedman, 1966). This is not to say that the residents are unaware that they live in the midst of death. That would simply not be possible, given that so many among them die. But their awareness of the hard, cold fact of death, as opposed to their strong awareness of finitude, is probably somewhat buffered by this geographical segregation of the terminally ill.

Perhaps the most important of the Forum-initiated activities is a "corridor-chairman" system. For each corridor in the village, the Forum appoints one individual to act as "den-mother." This person makes live or telephone contact with each resident on his or her corridor each day, and can mobilize formal and informal community supports when needed. Attempts are made to incorporate isolates, and particular watchfulness is paid to situations of potential crisis, such as bereavement over a spouse or friend. The system serves to define the atmosphere of the community as one of mutual support. As one resident put it, when a spouse dies, "people rally round—make dates for lunch with them."[5]

The majority of residents approve the low-key management of death and grief. In the words of one, "Here we are in the midst of death, so to speak, because you see notices often. I think death is very philosophically treated here." The philosophical treatment of death at Glen Brae rests, however, on a foundation of informal resident interaction.

The administration requires residents to make plans for their own deaths. They must have wills, designated executors, and specific plans for disposition of their bodies. This, however, is the only concrete way in which the administration itself positively intervenes in the ways residents deal with impending death. They have themselves taken other steps—meetings with the medical staff of the infirmary which led to agreements allowing the absence of heroic measures in sustaining life, as an example.

The residents of Glen Brae have developed a system of mutual supports and normative patterns of behavior toward death. Residents see death and, as with residents of most retirement villages, which are initially populated in "batches" when the community begins (Carp, 1972; Rosow, 1966), they are aware of the rising death rate as their overall population ages. Seeing other members of their community die, and thinking about their own impending deaths, they can draw on the informal supports available in their community. Glen Brae is organized to provide such assistance, by encouraging a high level of social interaction and by treating death informally.

Thus, death is neither a taboo topic, nor ritually separated from life. It is planned for, but it is also taken for granted and philosophically accepted. The situation is different from that at St. Joseph's, where individuals do not make specific plans for their dying, other than spiritual plans, and where they do not organize themselves as a community of the dying.

## LEGITIMIZING DEATH

Socialization for any aspect of aging is not highly programmed within our society. We have no rites of passage to mark the transition to old age, beyond the perfunctory retirement ritual which, in any case, affects few people making the transition into old age (Crawford, 1973). There are few specialized teachers or programs to prepare people for any aspect of old age (Ross, 1974; Rosow, 1974). Socialization for impending death is no exception to the general inadequacies of aging socialization, yet the anticipation of impending death poses a critical marginal situation for the individual (Berger and Luckmann, 1967: 97). As Hochschild (1973: 85) suggests, "Death is significant to the old in a way it is not to the young, not only because they are nearer to their own death but because they are nearer to other people's." Attaining a view of one's impending death as appropriate, legitimate, and acceptable can be viewed as either a personal or social construction of reality process, in which one's life, as it draws to a close in death, is rendered meaningful.

Impending death was not, on the whole, successfully legitimized by the residents of St. Joseph's, whereas it generally was at Glen Brae. A number of observations and interview responses suggest that, at St. Joseph's, the principal attitude to impending death was one of resignation, usually phrased in terms of relatively nonabstract religious formulae. When it comes to death, in the words of one, "Nobody's the boss but the Lord." Another, asked when she thinks about death, replied "I have nothing to say about that. If I die I'm going to die and there's nothing to it. I know I'm getting older and the day's shorter. But I don't worry about it." Others say, "The time is pre-destined," and, "You are just living until the Good Lord's ready to take you. You're going to die anyway. What's the difference." Impending death had no positive value attributed to it. People were willing either to die or to live longer if it was "God's will;" but death was not actively prepared for: "Don't plan for death because that's a sin. The Lord plans, not me."

One resident told me, "I'd say about 90% here are very morbid about death." I think this was an overstatement; rather, they were resigned to death because it would provide a release from present discomforts. As one resident said: "Well, I've seen people here wish they were gone. Your life can get so miserable and helpless they even pray for it." Another resident answered the question, "Would you agree or disagree with the statement, 'Death is sometimes a blessing?' " in general terms, but terms which exactly described his particular situation and that of most of his fellow-residents:

> Sometimes it is. Very much so if the person is poor—no friends or relations, no bankroll. What could you do. If you go into an old folk's home and you take this and take that and can't eat meals to your taste.

And another old man said:

> We old—no good no more . . . when you be old you see you no good no more. Best thing to go away [that is, die] . . . I don't want to live no more I say, I can't eat anything. I can't drink anything. I got to watch myself.

For him, to die was to suffer, but to live was to suffer more.

Both Glen Brae and St. Joseph's are places where people go to die. But at Glen Brae the accent is on living while at St. Joseph's it is on dying. In a sense, indeed, as noted above, the residents of St. Joseph's are already dead—that is, socially dead. As Kalish (1965) notes:

Social death occurs when an individual is thought of as dead and treated as dead, although he remains medically and legally alive. Any given person may be socially dead to one individual, to many individuals, or to virtually everyone, and perhaps to himself as well.

In short, "The self-perceived socially dead individual has accepted the notion that he is 'as good as dead,' or that he is, for all practical purposes, dead" (Kalish, 1968). And this, as Kalish notes, frequently occurs when a person enters a nursing home or a hospital, knowing he will not leave. Most St. Joseph's residents are largely or completely severed from family contact. They have low levels of contact with each other within the institution, and—while defined as medically alive by staff—they are frequently treated as if socially and psychologically (senile) dead.

One old man provided me with an insightful vignette which seems to capture the attitude of many. It was the day of a funeral, and he said:

I was talking with a guy this morning and I said when you get to be 70 you should die. He said no he wanted to live. I said, "What for? You produce anything? You bring home bread and butter? Better you die."

I have elsewhere (Marshall, 1975) argued the case that death is relatively successfully legitimated at Glen Brae. There, residents spoke to me as investigator with ease about death and dying generally and about their own. (This was much less the case at St. Joseph's.) A number of attitudinal indicators, if viewed in a "language-game"[6] (Simko, 1970; Winch, 1958; Wittgenstein, 1953, 1965) or "vocabulary of motive" (Mills, 1940) framework, provide evidence that the residents of that community have developed and share a number of good reasons why their death is appropriate or legitimate. To summarize briefly some interview data (see Marshall, 1975, for more extensive treatment), 91% of a sample of 79 do not feel that death is tragic for the person who dies; 98% say that death is sometimes a blessing; and only 12% say that death always comes too soon. These responses are much more accepting of death than is the pattern from a representative U.S. opinion survey which raised the same questions (Riley, 1970).[7]

There is additional evidence that a large proportion of the residents of Glen Brae feel that death is likely to come, for them, not too soon but too late. Asked both how long they anticipated living and how long they desired to live, only one-sixth expressed a desire to live longer than they anticipated living. That is, for the majority for whom data are available, death is expected to come either too late or just on time. In additional ways difficult to describe to others, they conveyed to me, during fieldwork and during formal interviewing sessions, a clear impression that they had reached a stage of their lives in which they could feel their impending death was appropriate.

## ORGANIZATIONAL FEATURES

Glaser and Strauss (1971: 116) point out that a person can go through a status passage alone, "as a member of a *cohort* that develops a collective or group character, or . . . as a member of an *aggregate* that has minimal collective features." Congregate residential facilities for the aged provide the possibility for either of the last two types of dying status passage. The cases discussed illustrate these alternatives. The issue is one of the extent to which passagees exert some control over their style of life while in passage (Glaser and Strauss, 1971: 64) and the relationship between in-passage control and the anticipations of the end of the passage.

Glen Brae is an organizational milieu where residents develop a shared perspective in dealing with their status passage. Examples of similar development of shared perspective, of course, abound in the literature of sociology (for example, Becker et al., 1961 and 1968; Olesen and Whittaker, 1968; Roth, 1963). St. Joseph's Home, on the other hand, provides an instance where passagees exert little collective control over their life style while in passage. Their passages are traversed in aggregate rather than collective fashion. They do not actively contribute to the development of their own subculture or status passage characteristics.

Let me make this distinction clearer by turning to Becker's (1964) analysis of personal change in adult life:

> A group finds itself sharing a common situation and common problems. Various members of the group experiment with possible solutions to those problems and report their experiences to their fellows. In the course of collective discussion, the members of the group arrive at a definition of the situation, its problems and possibilities, and develop consensus as to the most appropriate and efficient ways of behaving.

This consensus, definition, or subculture can be one in which the inevitable passage toward death is rendered meaningful or legitimate, but it need not develop in that way. A principal vehicle for creating any culture is conversation. As Berger and Kellner (1964) remark:

> The plausibility and stability of the world, as socially defined, is dependent upon the strength and continuity of significant relationships in which conversation about this world can be continually carried on . . . the reality of the world is sustained through conversation with significant others.

At Glen Brae the comparatively well-educated residents utilized high verbal skills in conversation, talking of death as a collective concern. At St. Joseph's, the overall amount of talk, as well as the amount of talk about death, was low. For example, when I asked residents whether people here often talk about losing loved ones through death, the typical reply was a flat, "No," or "I don't bother talking."

Of fundamental importance in the contrast between the two settings is the fact that the overall level of interaction, which is a precondition of conversation, differed so greatly. I have suggested that there is little activity at St. Joseph's[8] and that most of that which does occur is structured by staff. Staff imputations of disability may play a further role in structuring

and reducing both staff-resident and resident-resident interaction. Staff sometimes used the phrase, "They're just like
children, you know," in discussing residents. More than once I
was advised by a staff member "not to bother" to interview a
particular resident or patient, because "He's much too senile;
you won't be able to talk with him." While true in some cases, I
frequently found that I had already spoken with the resident,
carried on a somewhat difficult conversation, and gathered
useful data of a verbal nature. This imputation of senility, and
its interactional consequence, is not just a staff phenomenon:

> At lunch, Mrs. Brown said, "I see you talked with Miss Harrison. Be
> careful of what she said. She's senile, you know" [field notes].

On the whole, the attitude of staff toward patients and
residents was marked by a benevolent maternalism, as the
"just-like-children" remark indicates, or as is evident in a
nursing assistant's characterization of her patients: "They're all
babies. They all need care. They like to be babied." This
attitude leads staff to adopt a pattern of high control over the
status passagees.[9] As Glaser and Strauss (1971: 120) point out,
one tactic of socialization agents who wish to retain control
over passagees is to attempt to reduce communication among
them. At St. Joseph's the administration seeks to socialize
passagees for impending death through the use of formal ritual
(funerals), while a high degree of control is manifest over other
aspects of their lives.

At Glen Brae, while the administration makes no formal
attempts to socialize passagees for impending death, neither
does it seek to exert control over other aspects of the residents'
lives. This leaves them free to develop their own ways of dealing
with death as a community phenomenon.


## CONCLUSION

Some tentative conclusions of a more general nature emerge.
The vivid presence of death does not in itself lead to acceptance

of it. Dying is a status passage, and among the features of any status passage are the extent to which the actions of participants are regulated by others, the amount of control which the participants exercise, and whether the passage is traversed alone or with others (Glaser and Strauss, 1971: 8-9). An administration can allow passagees to exercise a high degree of status passage control, or it can seek to retain control.

At St. Joseph's Home, administrative practices mitigate against interaction so as to create the conditions for death to be faced without community support. Death is both geographically and ritually present at St. Joseph's Home, but positive acceptance of it is minimal. The trajectories of dying, as defined in the Home, serve to deny the reality that all are dying, for the definition is reserved for the very final stages, and leads to increased geographical isolation of the "dying" person on the infirmary floor or in St. Peter's Room. Funeral ritual, as employed in the Home, is formal and fails to involve the other community members in any meaningful way, as is evident from the switch possible from funeral in the morning to birthday party in the afternoon. At St. Joseph's, death has the character of something other than and outside of the individual. Because the organization for death and dying is provided for the residents and not by them, opportunities to construct the meaningfulness of dying are constrained.

At Glen Brae, residents deal with death as a community event. They take the initiative, in the absence of administrative initiatives, in recognizing their mutual terminal status passage, in creating its shape, and in fashioning its character. They make plans for death, and they have developed informal tacit understandings by which to deal with it. As a result, Glen Brae is a community setting where the residents are remarkably successful in legitimating their impending deaths. Highly important in this respect is the interactional and conversational foundation of community life. Low-keyed and resourceful, the residents have developed community control over the dying status passage.

The major organizational factor differentiating the two communities is the degree of resident-initiated social organization for death and dying. Death is frequent, visible, and ritually acknowledged at St. Joseph's Home, but it does not become a matter in which the residents, as members of a community, become involved. Death is frequent, visible, and informally dealt with by residents themselves at Glen Brae, where it becomes a focus of mutual status passage control and collective community involvement.

## NOTES

1. This draws heavily on Wilbert Moore (1963). Lyman and Scott (1970: 195) refer to the pace and sequencing of activities, while Roth (1963: 107-114) emphasizes the negotiated character of timetables in a way complementary to Glaser and Strauss' (1971) emphasis on status passage negotiation, which I discuss later.

2. Interestingly, however, those very few residents who were most active were presented to me and other outsiders as exemplary residents.

3. Observing this phenomenon one evening, I decided to find out what was happening with those residents not at the bingo game. In a darkened, second-floor lounge, I found eight or ten sitting quietly watching a television set. The picture was flipping.

4. Townsend (1962: 95) found an average yearly death rate of 17% in his survey of all homes for the aged and nursing homes in England and Wales.

5. St. Joseph's does not present this possibility because there are no married couples living there.

6. Theoretically, I treat certain language occurrences as demonstrating facility with a particular language-game centering on the giving of answers to questions (Wittgenstein, 1965: 67-68), such as interview questions about the appropriateness of each. Methodologically, I participated in such language-games with the subjects in order to make inferences as to their competencies in the language-game of death (see Simko, 1970). Winch (1958: 15) provides a link to the social construction of reality: "Our idea of what belongs to the realm of reality is given for us in the language that we use. The concepts we have settle for us the form of the experience we have of the world."

7. The results are also indicative of higher acceptance of impending death than was found from the small and unrepresentative number of residents of St. Joseph's to whom I put the same questions. Some of the verbatim responses appear earlier in this paper. At St. Joseph's I relied much more exclusively on participant observation, and informal discussion with residents, conducting only nine formal interviews over the five-month period during which I was in the field there.

8. It has been suggested that lower-class people are "reluctant to meet new people . . . to form new social relationships, and above all to initiate interaction with strangers" (Cohen and Hodges, 1963). It has also been argued that members of the lower classes have less facility and fluidity with language (e.g., Bernstein, 1960). While I would not with certainty rule out these possible explanations for the difference between Glen Brae and St. Joseph's, recent studies have demonstrated a high degree of interaction among aged working-class residents of a trailer park (Johnson, 1971), and a high-rise apartment building (Hochschild, 1973). Hochschild notes that the working-class aged she studied taught each other about death (1973: 79): "It was a fact of life . . . and there was no taboo against talk about it. . . . Although each individual faced death essentially alone, there was a collective concern with, as they put it, 'being ready' and facing up."

9. It is beyond the scope of this paper to go into the causes or origins of the organizational patterns in either setting. I suggest, however, that the rigid administrative control of St. Joseph's has a great deal to do with the fact that its clientele has little power. Organizational features in agencies serving powerless clientele tend, I suspect, to evolve in accordance with administrative convenience as a major criterion. For example, as a researcher "guest," I was provided by staff with coffee on demand. No residents had coffee or tea breaks between meals, because staff felt *some* of them could not handle the cups.

## REFERENCES

ALDRIDGE, G. (1956) "The role of older people in a Florida retirement community." Geriatrics 11: 223-226.

BECKER, H. (1964) "Personal change in adult life." Sociometry 27 (March): 40-53.

———, B. GEER, and E. HUGHES (1968) Making the Grade. New York: John Wiley.

——— and A. STRAUSS (1961) Boys in White. Chicago: Univ. of Chicago Press.

BERGER, P. and H. KELLNER (1964) "Marriage and the construction of reality." Diogene 46: 3-32.

BERGER, P. and T. LUCKMANN (1967) The Social Construction of Reality. Garden City: Doubleday-Anchor.

BERNSTEIN, B. (1960) "Language and social class." British J. of Sociology 11: 271-276.

CARP, F. (1972) "Mobility among members of an established retirement community." Gerontologist 12 (Spring): 48-56.

COHEN, A. and H. HODGES (1963) "Lower-blue-collar characteristics." Social Problems 10 (Spring): 303-334.

CRAWFORD, M. (1973) "Retirement: a rite de passage." Soc. Rev. 21, 3: 447-461.

FRIEDMAN, E. (1966) "Friendship choice and clique formation in a home for the aged." Ph.D. dissertation, Yale University.

GLASER, B. and A. STRAUSS (1971) Status Passage. Chicago: Aldine Atherton.

——— (1968) Time for Dying. Chicago: Aldine.

GOFFMAN, E. (1961) "On the characteristics of total institutions," pp. 1-24 in E. Goffman, Asylums. Garden City: Doubleday-Anchor.

GUSTAFSON, E. (1972) "Dying: the career of the nursing home patient." J. of Health & Social Behavior 13 (September): 226-235.

HOCHSCHILD, A. (1973) The Unexpected Community. Englewood Cliffs, N.J.: Prentice-Hall.

JOHNSON, S. (1971) Idle Haven. Berkeley: Univ. of California Press.

KALISH, R. (1968) "Life and death: dividing the indivisible." Social Science & Medicine 2: 249-259.

――― (1965) "The aged and dying process: the inevitable decisions." J. of Social Issues 21 (October): 87-96.

KALSON, L. (1972) "The therapy of independent living for the elderly." J. of the Amer. Geriatrics Society 20: 394-397.

LYMAN, S. and M. SCOTT (1970) "On the time track," pp. 189-212 in S. Lyman and M. Scott, A Sociology of the Absurd. New York: Appleton-Century-Crofts.

MARSHALL, V. (1975) "Socialization for impending death in a retirement village." Amer. J. of Sociology 80 (March): 1124-1144.

――― (1973) "Game-analyzable dilemmas in a retirement village: a case study." International J. of Aging & Human Development 4, 4: 285-291.

MESSER, M. (1967) "Possibility of an age-concentrated environment becoming a normative system." Gerontologist 17 (Winter): 247-251.

MILLS, C. W. (1940) "Situated actions and vocabularies of motive." Amer. Soc. Rev. 5: 904-913.

MOORE, W. (1963) Man, Time, and Society. New York: John Wiley.

OLESEN, V. and E. WHITTAKER (1968) The Silent Dialogue. San Francisco: Jossey-Bass.

RILEY, J. (1970) "What people think about death," pp. 30-41 in O. Brim, Jr., H. Freeman, S. Levine and N. Scotch (eds.) The Dying Patient. New York: Russell Sage.

ROSOW, I. (1974) Socialization to Old Age. Berkeley: Univ. of California Press.

――― (1966) "Discussion following Maurice B. Hamovitch's paper," pp. 127-135 in F. Carp (ed.) The Retirement Process. Washington, D.C.: U.S. Public Health Service Pub. No. 1778.

ROSS, J-K. (1974) "Learning to be retired: socialization into a French retirement residence." J. of Gerontology 29, 2: 211-223.

ROTH, J. (1963) Timetables. Indianapolis: Bobbs-Merrill.

SEGUIN, M. (1973) "Opportunity for peer socialization in a retirement community." Gerontologist 13 (Summer): 208-214.

SIMKO, A. (1970) "Death and the hereafter: the structuring of immaterial reality." Omega 1 (May): 121-135.

SUDNOW, D. (1967) Passing On: The Social Organization of Dying. Englewood Cliffs, N.J.: Prentice-Hall.

TOWNSEND, P. (1962) The Last Refuge. London: Routledge & Kegan Paul.

WINCH, P. (1958) The Idea of a Social Science and its Relations to Philosophy. London: Routledge & Kegan Paul.

WITTGENSTEIN, L. (1965) The Blue and Brown Books. New York: Harper & Row (Torchbook ed.).

――― (1953) Philosophical Investigations (G. Anscombe, trans.). New York: Macmillan.

*JUANITA WOOD* is a Ph.D. candidate at the University of California, Davis. Her major interests are in social interaction, collective behavior and medical sociology.

# THE STRUCTURE OF CONCERN:

*The Ministry in Death-Related Situations*

## JUANITA WOOD

THIS REPORT is an examination of how ministers fulfill that part of their role encompassing death work; how the minister as death worker functions. More concretely, the report entails a close examination of one component of ministerial death work which the ministers feel is important: the expression of concern.

For those ministers studied, the dying or grief situation was viewed as serious, as problematic, and as in need of management. Death situations elicit concern and, in turn, are situations in which one expresses concern. These death workers feel the expression of concern is a necessary element of the death worker role. One minister relates his first priority upon entering a death scene: "I think first of all you have to show compassion, that you care, and proceed from there with some kind of counsel from the scriptures." It is a working assumption that, when someone is dying or grieving, others should be concerned and that this concern is helpful: "then just the idea of recognizing that, just showing concern and letting the person show some feelings and me express some feelings . . . this in itself does a great deal."

Setting aside the question of whether or not expressions of concern are in fact helpful, the sociologically more interesting question of how concern is shown might then be asked. How does one structure an expression of concern? What are its elements? In other words, when a minister wishes to demonstrate concern for another person, what does he mean and how does he do it? To begin to suggest answers to these questions, it is necessary first to examine just what these ministers *qua* death workers do, and only then to offer tentative explanations for their action.

This report is based on an intensive interview study of 31 male ministers in two different communities.[1] Interviews ranged from one to two hours in length and were composed of open-ended questions covering three death work areas: (1) the dying patient, (2) the funeral, and (3) the bereaved. The discussion in this report is confined to the dying patient and the bereaved.

## *SITUATIONAL AMBIGUITY*

Opening the door and entering a hospital room in which someone is dying or confronting a newly or potentially bereaved person can be an unnerving experience for a minister: he may lack information about the person and knowledge about how that person feels about the medical prognosis or the death, about whether the person knows the prognosis, about how he might best serve, or about how the person feels about ministers. The minister may also have his own personal fears of death. There are many possible contributors to the unnerving experience, but they primarily revolve around one theme—uncertainty. The minister is uncertain about the proper procedure, what expectations are held relative to his behavior, and what the consequences of any given action might be. There is confusion as to what kind of concern is proper. One minister relates this feeling of ambiguity:

Well, sometimes you walk into things [and] you don't know what they want. See, if you're a psychiatrist and people come in, you have a contract. If you're a minister, you can wind up with anything from a group therapy session to an outburst of anger. It depends on what's going on. A lot of times the situation is unknown.

There is, of course, a reduction of uncertainty as knowledge of the actors and/or the specifics of the situation increases, but for many calls, initial knowledge is very scanty:

In many cases, and I'm sure this is true for many ministers, you're called into the situation where the people have no church. You don't know them from Adam. You know nothing about them. And usually you're notified after by the funeral home or someone, and you don't know anything about the situation, and the person's already dead.

The lack of information, then, creates unease and impels the minister to develop a method of searching for information that will render the situation less ambiguous.

### *LISTENING*

In the initial contact period, the minister is often concerned with how best to conduct himself so that (1) order is maintained, (2) interaction is made possible, and (3) he is able to feel that he has been of some help. But in an ambiguous situation how is this to be done? How is it possible to manage a situation and to show concern, especially if personal knowledge is lacking?[2] Let us step back for a moment and view briefly what is going on in the larger social world at this time that might have a bearing on these questions.

As our society has moved from the emphasis on exchange based on commodities to an emphasis on exchange based on services,[3] we have seen a rise in the number of professional counselors.[4] These professionals, working within a psycho-logistic, person-oriented framework, have been very effective in influencing our conceptions of what one does when one wants to help someone in a difficult situation—so much so that most of us have a basic working knowledge of the importance of, for example, encouraging the person to express feelings, reflecting statements back to them, being nonjudgmental, and listening.[5] These techniques have become part of our everyday, getting-through-the-world routine. They are ways of dealing with and making predictable those situations in which we usually experience unease. They give us a way to structure our concern; a sort of "how-to-do-it" formula for when we want to help, but don't know what to do.

Secondly, in our linear culture we conceptualize life and events as progressing from point to point or from stage to stage. Life is a process which develops, and life events are in constant motion.[6] Both in physical health and mental health we expect certain illnesses to follow along certain lines as they progress. Glaser and Strauss (1965: 52), for example, note the medical importance of the staff working with the dying patient knowing which stage or "status" the patient is in:

> Accompanying this passage is an important change in the goals of nursing care: that from working hard to recover the patient to routinely providing him comfort until death. If nurses perceive the passage inaccurately they can cease trying to save a patient, although he still may have a chance to survive.

Responses may also be geared to the perceived emotional condition of the patient, although doctors are less concerned with this than are nurses. Simmons and Given (1972: 219) in their article on nursing the terminally ill, note:

> If one is to provide comfort and treat the patient as an individual, he must know the patient's concerns and attitudes toward the illness and death. The nurse must determine the patient's stage of awareness so that the response is appropriate.

The underlying assumption is that of a continuum along which the patient is passing and care is adjusted to reflect the perceived need of each particular point along the way.

The third point that needs to be mentioned here is the influence of the Kubler-Ross (1969) book on the care and treatment of the dying patient, in which she identified five emotional stages through which the dying progress before death. The book made a considerable impact on both medical personnel and counselors and triggered subsequent publications which also delineated stages.[7] Perhaps one reason for the great impact of the book was the fact that it fit neatly into our mode of linear thinking. More importantly, it also fit into the prevalent counseling pattern of the day with the emphasis on finding "where the person is at."

What I want to emphasize here, then, is that our culture provides us with a concept of progression, a current strong counseling ethos in which we are concerned with emotional expression of feelings, and with published works which point out specific emotional stages through which people progress in death-related situations. The ministers, none of whom have received explicit, detailed training as death workers, but who are familiar with counseling techniques, are able to draw on these current cultural techniques to order their own work.

Thus it is that nondirective listening becomes the minister's basic technique. Efforts are made to "open the person up," to "see where they're at." The emphasis is on encouraging the person to be verbally expressive so that the minister may listen for cues as to how he or she perceives the situation. One way to do this is to use simple, direct questions.

> I went in and she greeted me and I sat and she looked like she was thinking very profoundly—a bit pained in her expression—and I simply said to her, "Barbara, you look as if you are thinking very deeply and feeling very deeply right now." And she said, "I am." I said, "Can you tell me what about?" And she said, "About what I have to face." And then so it could be open to be dealt with explicitly, I said, "And what's that?" And she said, "My dying." And that opened it up to talk about her feelings.

Another method is to probe for feelings.

> Well, I guess again there you're trying to pick up on the feelings and you get a routine answer, you know, "I'm fine," and then maybe you just talk small talk for a while just to get more feelings—just how the person really seems to be doing. Whether the person is downcast or discouraged or feeling happy. . . . and then sometimes we'll ask again in a different way how they're feeling.

Reflection is yet another technique. Still others conceive of their listening style much more passively and "wait to be led by the patient and not the other way around."

Through relatively nondirective listening, the minister is able to begin to gather cues as to what the appropriate response seems to be and what type of concern seems called for. For example, circumstances may seem to require taking control of the situation or serving as a behavior model when emotional outbursts are anticipated and viewed as a threat to order. One minister indicates:

> If people don't have a firmness or someone strong in charge or in control at this particular time, they'll fall apart, some people will, because they don't have enough internal control, so they need an external control saying, "That's it."

Or the situation may be viewed as one in which the person needs someone to talk with or pray with. The minister listens to assess what he thinks will be most helpful.

## AVAILABILITY

In addition to situational ambiguity, ministers have another somewhat unique problem: they are potentially available to anyone who asks for their services. In many instances they are accessible without appointment. The nature of the pastoral role as a helping role makes availability unavoidable. One minister explains, "Part of my role is to try to help where there is a need; and if that need is there, then that is part of my role." If one is potentially available to everyone, the problem, when allocating time, of making distinctions about which situations are more important necessarily arises. The minister, as all of us do, has only so much time to allocate in each day so that the giving of proper attention may become problematic.

Some counseling situations, especially death-related ones, may require more of a time investment than others. When questioned as to the length of the hospital visits to the dying, one minister replied:

> It varies a great deal, but maybe 10-15 minutes. It could be longer and often is. . . . with people that are terminally ill you would probably spend a little more time than with other calls because you're more concerned, obviously. You make a point of being available—more available than if the person is just sick.

In addition to gauging the seriousness of the situation, the minister must also gauge the number of other commitments on any given day. Commenting on a woman who asked him to call on her, one relates:

> When I went in and sat down she asked me if I wanted a cup of coffee. It usually takes people about 20 minutes to get around to the point unless you do the obvious thing. After about 10 minutes, I started looking at my watch and, of course, she panicked and, of course, I wanted her to because I don't have hours to sit around.

His being available to everyone on an on-call basis oftentimes generates the use of the minister in a merely perfunctory way by people outside his congregation. This further necessitates the minister's adoption of those means which are apparently most efficient for meeting the demands placed on his time. One pastor recalls his experience as a junior pastor in a large church:

> Because I was doing so many [funerals] in southern California, I, quite frankly, had two or three services I wrote that I liked and used so I had them mimeographed with only blank spaces left for names and that kind of thing. This may seem terribly impersonal, but I was overwhelmed by the amount of time it would take otherwise. And I always had the opportunity to personalize it a little bit, and I always did.

Here is but one illustration of the classic ministerial dilemma: how does one structure concern so as to make it personal and, at the same time, make the most efficient use of one's time?

Given such constraints and given the ambiguous nature of many situations, listening tends to become selective, reducing the requisite time for determining correct responses. As will be seen in the following section, ministers listen not only in a nondirective, but also in a highly selective, manner. But what they listen *for* is influenced by their personal orientations to the ministry.

## HUMANISTS VERSUS TRADITIONALISTS

Here I need to make a very rudimentary classification. The ministers I interviewed seemed to orient themselves in one of two ways relative to their view of themselves and their work: (1) as humanists, or (2) as traditionalists. By humanist, I mean that those who place themselves in this category tend to identify with the psychological counselor image. The traditionalists, on the other hand, tend to identify with the paternal guidance image. Each is listening for different kinds of cues, and for each group "being open" is interpreted in a different way.

For "humanistic" ministers, the important information to extract is in what "stage" the dying or grieving person is. These ministers, already equipped with psychologically oriented counseling training, have generally adopted Kübler-Ross' dying stages or some variant of them as a paradigm in working with the dying and bereaved. One minister responded to the question of what cues one looks for in the following manner:

> I have certain conceptualizations to begin with about what the meaning of dying is that would provide me with a framework for cues to look for, and I would assume that if people are told of this they are going to go through a period of shock and it's just not going to register, and then they're going to go through a period in which they're going to be good and irritable or disturbed ... period of depression, and very gradually a resolution of it.

While this particular minister exemplifies more explicitly than most the assumption of Kübler-Ross' five stages, other humanist ministers also assume the existence of such stages.

The traditionalist ministers, in contrast, search for the degree of spiritual commitment. One explains his concern:

> I will try to find out where they are in their relationship with Christ. If they don't know anything at all, I have a gospel presentation, not a sermon, but I'll choose one simple presentation of the gospel that tells how you can have a personal relationship with Jesus Christ. If this person is a Christian, I will just go into some of the scriptures to give that person a firm grip on what they already believe.

Other traditional ministers comment on their ministry being effective when a person is "open to some spiritual counseling." Thus, for this group, openness is associated with the person's willingness to verbally *share a belief* in the word of God as presented in the Bible.

For the humanist group, openness is associated with the person's willingness to verbalize emotions and to *share feelings* with the minister.

Individual orientation on the part of the minister, then, dictates what it is important to be concerned *about.* In the one instance selective listening occurs to detect degree of spiritual commitment; in the other, one listens for location along a stage continuum.

## CONCERN CONSTRUCTION

It is now possible to speak of a process of concern construction that, simply put, contains the following steps: (1) gathering of relayed information, (2) gathering of situational information, (3) reducing ambiguity, and (4) scheduling concern. The first three steps have been included in what has been discussed above, but will be briefly summarized below. The last is a consequence of the first three and is perhaps the most important, for it· is through scheduling concern that the experience of death and grief are defined for both the minister and the dying or grieving person.

*Gathering of relayed information:* Before the minister makes contact with either a dying or bereaved person, information on the situation is usually relayed to him by others—family members, church members, friends, medical staff, funeral directors, etc. This information may be more or less detailed, but it does give the minister some means of gauging the seriousness of the impending encounter, some personal information about the individual and about what kinds of ties or support he has, and so forth. At this point the minister can begin to formulate an approach to the situation.

*Gathering of situational information:* Once contact is made, the minister begins to gather more information from the person involved. Such indicators as physical condition, responsiveness, manner of speaking, and so on, become cues for the minister to respond to. But uncertainty as to what is "really" indicated in the situation remains. Situations are unpredictable, in part, because of ministerial anticipation of variance in individual reactions to extreme stress. The minister simply does not, in many cases, know what to expect. What is needed then is a method of reducing the ambiguity.

*Reduction of ambiguity:* This is accomplished by drawing on those methods used in other counseling situations which are thought to be effective—getting the person to talk, to express feelings, to share. In this way the minister is able to begin to decide how he can most effectively manage the situation. A definition can be formed as to what the person "needs." Through listening, the minister is able to determine where the person "is" within the particular progression he is looking for and thus what "needs" to be done. The traditional minister listens for evidence of degree of relationship with Christ. The humanistic minister listens for evidence of emotional stage currently being traversed.

*Scheduling concern:* When the minister engages in selective listening, he is in fact limiting what will be recognized as appropriate to the situation. If one accepts, for example, that a dying person progresses from denial to anger to bargaining to depression to acceptance, any statement made or behavior exhibited by the person may be interpreted to correspond with one of these stages. The same is true in the traditional sphere where, as we have seen, statements and behavior are taken as indicating some degree of relationship with Christ and concomitant readiness to accept God's will. That is, concern is "scheduled" according to "where" the minister perceives the person to be.

Selective listening and scheduled concern, then, come to define what the experience of death and grief are. By recognizing and validating some experiences over others, those so excluded become irrelevant. One minister illustrates this point:

> Sometimes I think just letting a person discover his own problem by just talking with him is not the best way because I think sometimes we can share with them, "This is your real problem." Maybe bitterness, "You have all these surface problems, but your main problem is bitterness, and if you want to face up to it you can. If you don't, you're going to continue to have all these problems."

The minister defines both the present and the anticipated experience for the passer. He may determine not only what category one is in, i.e., "you are feeling bitter," but also the amount of time appropriate to spend in each. One minister relates that when he feels grief has gone on too long:

> I say, "That's enough." I say, "Now look, this is long enough. You need to come out of it and you need to get ahold of yourself and you need to get out and associate with people, and not only do you need to, you must."

All of this has the effect of *delimiting* the minister's concern to only those emotions or experiences validated by the paradigm he is using.[8] This simplifies the dying process not only for him, but, hypothetically at least, for the dying and bereaved as well. It sets boundaries on what to listen for, be concerned about and, possibly, experience.

In addition to excluding feelings deemed inappropriate, many expressed feelings may simply not be recognized at all. It is not anticipated, for example, that the dying or bereaved may feel excitement, joy, or gratitude; and if a person does experience an unanticipated emotion, it is either skipped over or interpreted as indicating a working through of one or all of the stages, as in the following:

> In this particular situation, he didn't need to go through . . . like the denial or some of these things because he . . . was pretty much able to accept this and express his feelings and concerns. . . . In fact, in many ways this was an unusual situation because he was able to have worked this thing through—didn't have some of the problems other people would have had.

Once the minister feels the passer has reached the final stage, whether it be deep religious commitment or acceptance of the inevitability of death, then concern can be relaxed.

> We have a lady in a convalescent home here and I have one of the ladies go and read to her and I visit her occasionally, once every two weeks perhaps. She's a Christian lady and there's no need for any preparation for her to die—she's ready.

Concern is "scheduled" also in the sense of its expression being limited to discrete time periods. Most professional service workers in our modern era have adopted the appointment as a tool in serving the greatest number. Thus, we are all familiar with the necessity of making appointments with our doctors, dentists, psychiatrists, and so forth. And we are all committed—habituated is perhaps a better word—to the assumption that this is the most viable manner in which to operate—that the concern professionals have for us is necessarily limited and temporally bounded. In the world of the hospital, for example, medical concern is expressed in routinized times for checking temperatures, giving medication, bathing, and so forth. And with the new and growing interest in the medical field, in the proper personal treatment of the dying, we have nurses suggesting that it too be scheduled:

> The staff should know what problems face patients and plan their time in their care schedules to listen or help direct the patient's thoughts just as much as time is planned to give medications, do treatments, or chart [Simmons and Given, 1972: 220].

(In like manner, Threshold Research Center on Death and Dying, Inc., a newly established organization, has instituted a program in which a dying person may rent, by the hour, a companion to be with him or her.)[9] Among ministers, too, concern is scheduled in this temporal sense. That is, concern is constructed around a position determination relative to the passer and the expression of interest in either validating that position or encouraging the person to move on. But this validation or encouragement is of limited duration. Concern is broken into limited time segments.

In sum, then, scheduling concern involves:

(1) an attenuation of areas of concern: Concern is structured so as to encompass some experiences and not others. One is not simply concerned, but rather concerned only about specific predefined human experiences.

(2) an attenuation of attention: Once the area of concern is determined and concern expressed in that area, the attention period is over and leave-taking may begin:

> Well, it's always hard because they're hanging on, but I just say that I have other appointments, that I have to go to because there are people that have real problems and I have to see them. And I say, "You know how it felt when I came in, how you were able to receive comfort? Well, there's someone else waiting for the same thing." I've had people hang on and say, "You can't leave," and usually I stay longer when they do, but I break away as soon as I can and there's usually someone there taking care of them and I get to where they can't get ahold of my hand.

## CONCLUSION

I have noted the uncertainty of the minister's role as a death worker and the situational ambiguity that obtains. In the course of reducing this ambiguity, and in an effort to effectively manage the situation, I have noted the adoption by the minister of the current societal belief in person-centered therapy techniques, most particularly listening.

Time constraints and the utilization of a "stages" paradigm (however articulated) leads to a form of selective listening in which the minister manages and defines death-related situations. The process of selecting and excluding information, of defining and setting boundaries on what areas are relevant to concern may simplify the dying and grieving process for the dying and bereaved. It clearly does so for the minister. Concern need be shown—scheduled—only for specific, predefined components of the dying and grieving experience which are taken to be what dying and grief *are*. It is conceivable, however, that humans may experience feelings, emotions, and so forth, not included in the paradigm being used. The danger in listening not for where a person "is," but for where a person is within a *particular* framework, is simply that one may be referring to the wrong framework. Concern comes to be structured in reference to an anticipated stage rather than to the individual per se.

## NOTES

1. Female ministers were not excluded from my study. However, in the two communities there was only one woman minister, and she arrived subsequent to the data-gathering. For this reason, male pronouns are used throughout.

2. I am using the concept of personal knowledge in the same way as Lyn Lofland (1973) to include knowledge of biography as well as of roles and statuses.

3. See, for example, Halmos (1967) or Bell (1973).

4. According to Halmos (1966), as of 1960 there were 70,589 practicing professional counselors in the United States, and a rapid increase anticipated.

5. Evidence of this in nonprofessional spheres may be noted in such unexpected places as the Chevrolet dealer magazine, *Friends* (1974: 21), in which the technique of listening is commented on by one "service advisor":

One of the topics most interesting to me explained the value of those few moments the service advisor has with the customer when he drives in. The course not only explained how he should talk to a customer, but more importantly, *how to listen effectively* to the customer.

There is also James Foreman's (1973) interesting content analysis of funeral director's journal articles in 1905, 1939, and 1963, in which he noticed the changing orientations from sanitizing to naturalizing to sympathizing.

    6. For an elaboration of this point, see Dorothy Lee (1950).

    7. For example, Robert Kavanaugh (1972) designates seven stages of grief.

    8. Since the publication of Kubler-Ross' book, there are a growing number of criticisms along this line. See, for example, John Langone (1974), Edwin S. Shneidman (1973), and Warren Shibles (1974: 222-226).

    9. From an advertisement distributed by Threshold, Inc., 1100 Glendon Avenue, Suite 1725, Los Angeles, CA 90024.

# REFERENCES

BELL, D. (1973) The Coming of Post-Industrial Society: A Venture in Social Forecasting. New York: Basic Books.

Friends (1974) "Service management is a college course." Vol. 31 (September): 20-23.

FOREMAN, J. (1973) "Theory and the ideal type of the professional: the case of the funeral director." Omega 4 (Fall): 221-227.

GLASER, B. G. and A. L. STRAUSS (1965) "Temporal aspects of dying as a non-scheduled status passage." Amer. J. of Sociology 71 (July): 48-59.

GROLLMAN, E. A. (1974) Concerning Death: A Practical Guide for the Living. Boston: Beacon.

——— [ed.] (1966) Rabbinical Counseling. New York: Bloch.

HALMOS, P. (1970) The Personal Service Society. New York: Schocken.

——— (1967) "The personal service society." British J. of Sociology 18 (March): 13-27.

——— (1966) The Faith of the Counsellors. New York: Schocken.

KAVANAUGH, R. (1972) Facing Death. Los Angeles: Nash.

KUBLER-ROSS, E. (1974) Questions and Answers on Death and Dying. New York: Collier.

——— (1969) On Death and Dying. New York: Macmillan.

KUTSCHER, A. H. (1969) Death and Bereavement. Springfield, Ill.: Charles C Thomas.

LANGONE, J. (1974) Vital Signs. Boston: Little, Brown.

LEE, D. (1950) "Lineal and nonlineal codifications of reality." Psychosomatic Medicine 12 (March & April): 89-97.

LOFLAND, L. (1973) A World of Strangers. New York: Basic Books.

PATTISON, A. H. (1969) "Help in the dying process." Voices 5: 6-14.

PEARSON, L. [ed.] (1969) Death and Dying: Current Issues in the Treatment of the Dying Person. Cleveland: Press of Case Western Reserve Univ.

SHIBLES, W. (1974) Death: An Interdisciplinary Approach. Whitewater, Wis.: Language Press.

SHNEIDMAN, E. S. (1973) Deaths of Man. New York: Quadrangle.

SIMMONS, S. and B. GIVEN (1972) "Nursing care of the terminal patient." Omega 3 (August): 217-225.

SUDNOW, D. (1967) Passing On: The Social Organization of Dying. Englewood Cliffs, N.J.: Prentice-Hall.

WEISMAN, A. D. (1972) On Dying and Denying: A Psychiatric Study of Terminality. New York: Behavioral Publications.

VERNON, G. M. (1970) Sociology of Death: An Analysis of Death-Related Behavior. New York: Ronald Press.

**NOTES**

NOTES *107486*

| DATE DUE | | | |
|---|---|---|---|
| MAY 6 '90 | MAY 7 '80 | JUL 8 '81 | |
| JUL 8 '8 | JUL 8 '81 | | |
| OC 17 '84 | NOV 6 '84 | | |
| NO 27 '84 | DEC 6 '84 | | |
| NO 26 '90 | NOV 19 '90 | | |
| | | | |
| | | | |
| | | | |
| | | | |
| | | | |
| | | | |
| | | | |
| | | | |
| | | | |
| | | | |
| | | | |

DEMCO 38-297